HARVARD MIDDLE EASTERN MONOGRAPHS

XIII

THE ECONOMY OF THE
ISRAELI KIBBUTZ

BY

ELIYAHU KANOVSKY

DISTRIBUTED FOR THE

CENTER FOR MIDDLE EASTERN STUDIES

OF HARVARD UNIVERSITY BY

HARVARD UNIVERSITY PRESS

CAMBRIDGE, MASSACHUSETTS

1966

Second printing, 1966

LIBRARY OF CONGRESS CATALOG CARD NUMBER 66-18097

PRINTED IN THE UNITED STATES OF AMERICA

TO THE MEMORY OF MY MOTHER

PREFACE

There is a rather extensive literature dealing with the role of the Israeli kibbutzim as the vanguard of Zionist pioneering settlement prior to Israeli independence in 1948. There are many books, articles, and brochures describing the principles and ideology of the collectives; the unique socio-economic structure; the heroism of the pioneers; the system of child care and education and its results; the role of the woman in the communal set-up; the social security which the kibbutz affords its members and the "purity" of its democratic organization. Since 1948, many books and articles have been written by sociologists, educators, and other scholars analyzing the changes which Israeli independence has wrought. A careful scanning of the literature (most of which is in Hebrew) has revealed that very little has been written providing an objective, comprehensive analysis of the *economy* of the Israeli kibbutzim in the post-independence period. A few books and many articles have been written, but these are, in the opinion of this writer, either one-sided in their approach, or concern themselves with particular aspects of the collective economy rather than with the totality of the kibbutz economy. What was particularly striking and puzzling were the repeated claims that the collective economy was highly productive *and* the repeated demands for special financial aid from the Israeli government, the Jewish Agency, and the Histadrut. A priori, these claims and demands appeared to be contradictory.

The original draft of this monograph was written under the guidance of Professor Charles Issawi of Columbia University. Subsequently, a Research Fellowship provided by the Center for Middle Eastern Studies at Harvard University enabled a thorough revision and up-dating of the original draft in accordance with suggestions made by Professor Simon Kuznets of Harvard University, Professor A. J. Meyer, Associate Director of the Center for Middle Eastern Studies at Harvard University, Aharon Gilshon, Director of Agricultural Research at the Bank of Israel in Jerusalem, and many others both in the United States and in Israel who were kind enough to read the original manuscript and to offer constructive suggestions. I am most grateful to other individuals, too many to enumerate, in this country and in Israel, who offered their advice, and to the librarians at the Zionist Archives, who provided the necessary basic data, without which this study would have been impossible. I owe a special debt of gratitude to Professors Meyer and Issawi who painstakingly reviewed the manuscript and provided the necessary encouragement for its completion. Finally, the forbearance and understanding of my wife and children during all these years were indispensable.

E. K.

Brooklyn, New York
December 1965

CONTENTS

LIST OF TABLES

THE ECONOMY OF THE ISRAELI KIBBUTZ

INTRODUCTION

The kibbutzim (collective settlements) in Israel constitute a unique socio-economic structure unparalleled in any other part of the world. Their uniqueness consists of their complete collectivization both of production and consumption on a completely voluntary basis. However, they did not arise or develop in response to any preconceived plan, as did the various utopian societies which existed in many parts of the world. Furthermore, their members were not regarded as mere utopian visionaries; on the contrary — in the days prior to the establishment of the State of Israel in 1948 — they had a very considerable influence on the economic, social, political, and military development of the Jewish community in Palestine. Though their influence has waned since 1948, it still transcends their small percentage (3.6 per cent in 1964) of Israeli Jewry.

Although the ideology of the kibbutz movement is socialistic, it should be noted that the movement did not arise as a result of Marxist influence. Karl Marx was opposed to the "utopian" societies. In his opinion they deflected the revolutionary spirit of the "proletariat" from their political and economic aims, namely, the overthrow of the capitalist system. The first kibbutz was founded in 1909, and kibbutzim had been established before Stalin began his drive of forced collectivization of Russian agriculture in the 1930's. The Russian commune (similar in structure to the Israeli kibbutz) never succeeded. The Soviet kolkhoz system, which became the dominant form of Soviet agriculture, differs considerably from the kibbutz. In the kolkhoz, consumption of personal disposable income is private; in the kibbutz it is collective. Production in the kolkhoz consists of a small private sector, together with a larger collective sector; in the kibbutz all production is collective. In the kolkhoz, the members are paid in accordance with the number of work-days in the collective farm, the work-day of the skilled being more remunerative than that of the unskilled; in the kibbutz no member is "paid" — he and his family are provided for, regardless of his level of skills, or the number of his dependents. The kolkhoz is an agricultural enterprise; the kibbutz has a large mixture of non-agricultural activities. The kolkhoz is controlled and directed by government appointees; the kibbutz is truly democratic in character. Basically, the kolkhoz is one more unit of governmental enterprise (though legal title is in the hands of the kolkhoz members), while the kibbutz is an independent unit, competing with private enterprise. The Chinese communes seem to have a closer superficial resemblance to the kibbutz; however, they, too, arose and persist as a result of governmental compulsion and direction. Even the Ejido experiment of the Cardenas regime in Mexico in the 1930's was stimulated by considerable governmental inducements and was subject to special supervision, direction, and aid. With the passing of the Cardenas administration, few of the Ejidos remained. These settlements were closer in structure to the Soviet kolkhoz than to the Israeli kibbutz.[1]

Thus the kibbutzim are unique in their historical development, in their structure, and in their relationship with the society and economy of the country. The fact that the oldest kibbutz has been in existence for over fifty years is indicative of an internal stability persisting as far as the third generation.

Recent world history has seen the rise of many newly-independent countries, especially in Asia and Africa. These so-called underdeveloped countries have been in search of ways and means of raising their very low levels of national income, favoring neither the free enterprise system, as practiced in the United States today, nor the Communist system. They have been exploring ways of adapting what they consider to be the desirable features of both systems, without resorting to the degree of monolithic state control and direction typical of the Communist countries.

Delegates from the French Sudan, after visiting Israel, decided upon their return to set up an experimental collective settlement in the vicinity of their capital, and at their request, the Israeli government sent an agricultural counsellor to the Sudan. A group of fifty-six demobilized Burmese army officers and soldiers spent a year in Israel, training in cooperative and collective settlements for the purpose of establishing similar villages in their own country.[2] Ghana invited a cooperative settlement expert from Israel to aid in a study of the feasibility of setting up farm communities in Ghana patterned on the Israeli kibbutzim and moshavim.[3] At least one small kibbutz already exists in India, after an Indian had visited Israel and been much impressed by such a community.[4]

It is to be hoped that this study of the economy of the Israeli collectives — their successes and failures — will be not only informative, but of aid to those planning and executing economic development plans, in Israel as well as in other countries.

I

ISRAELI AGRICULTURE

Although the industrial sector is playing an increasingly important role within the kibbutzim, the majority of Israeli collectives and cooperatives are based mainly on agriculture. The following brief description of the major agricultural sectors — the moshav, the kibbutz, and private Jewish and Arab enterprises — will give the reader a clearer understanding of the kibbutz economy and its position within the economy of the country.

For a country about the size of New Jersey (approximately 8,000 square miles in area), the climatic, topographical, and geological variations are very considerable. The average annual rainfall varies from 16 to 24 inches in the coastal area, to 2 inches in the Dead Sea area and 1 inch in Eilat, the southernmost tip of Israel.[1]

Within the given natural conditions, the institutional patterns are of basic importance in determining the nature and tempo of development, and the relative success or failure of the various agricultural branches. Institutional patterns refer not only to the structure of the farms, the nature of ownership and operation, but also to the policies of the government, the Jewish Agency, and other public bodies.

THE MOSHAVIM

The moshav (pl. moshavim) constitutes the largest single agricultural sector. The moshavim are cooperative (not collective) settlements, organized on the basis of individual holdings of land, buildings, and smaller agricultural implements. There is a large measure of cooperation in marketing and purchasing, in the joint ownership of large agricultural machinery, and in the joint cultivation of certain crops. Most of the moshavim lease their land on a 49-year renewable-lease basis from the Jewish National

Fund, and receive the initial settlement budget from the Jewish Agency.[2]

The general plan of the moshav includes a central area with all the community buildings and services, such as cooperative stores and sales units, warehouses for major farm equipment, a school and synagogue, central executive offices, repair shops, as well as centers for other village services. Back of these communal buildings are the private homes and small plots with a barn and outbuildings for poultry and other domestic animals. Farther out are the farm plots of each moshav member. There are various mutual aid arrangements (provided by a tax on the moshav membership) for those in need as a result of serious illness or any other emergency. If necessary, loans are provided without danger of foreclosure. A member usually has the right to sell his property and leave the moshav, but the new buyer must meet the approval of the remaining members. Health services are provided (as in the kibbutzim) by the Kuppat Holim of the Histadrut (Federation of Jewish Labor).[3]

Though the first moshav, in its present form, was established shortly after the First World War, the greatest expansion of this form of settlement took place after Israeli independence in 1948. Its primacy in Israeli agriculture dates from the early 1950's. While the moshav was originally planned as a diversified farm, most of the older moshavim, and many of the newer ones, have evolved into specialized commercial farms, primarily for dairy and poultry, although some specialize in citriculture. Most of the newer moshavim (those established after 1948) are more diversified, with greater emphasis on vegetables and field crops. As of December 31, 1964, there were 346 moshavim with a population of 119,923 (including 356 non-Jewish residents). The bulk of these settlements had been established since Israel's independence in 1948. In Israel as a whole, the rural population as a percentage of the total has been declining in spite of official efforts on the part of the government and the Jewish Agency, and in spite of the higher birth rates in the rural areas. In 1964, 20.1 per cent of Israel's population was classified as rural, and within Israel's Jewish population 13.2 per cent lived in non-urban areas. The moshav sector constituted almost one-fourth of the total rural population and over 40 per cent of the Jewish rural population. In 1964, 12.9 per cent of Israel's labor force was employed in agriculture (including forestry and fisheries); among the Jews the percentage was 10.6. The moshavim provided a considerable share of this labor force. Unlike the kibbutz, which has tended to place an increasing emphasis on non-agricultural pursuits, the moshav remains a largely agricultural unit, with its ancillary services provided by a small number of settlers engaged in manufacturing or crafts. Some of the less successful farmers supplement their farm income by working in manufacturing establishments outside their settlements (see Table 1).

TABLE 1. THE KIBBUTZIM AND MOSHAVIM IN 1964

	MOSHAVIM	KIBBUTZIM
Number of settlements	346	230
Settlements established before Israel's independence	78	135
Population of these settlements	26,872	61,528
Settlements established after Israel's independence	268	95
Population of these settlements	93,051	19,411
Total population	119,923	80,939
Percentage of Israel's population	4.7	3.2
Percentage of Israeli Jewry	5.3	3.6
Percentage of Israel's rural population	23.6	15.9
Percentage of Israel's Jewish rural population	40.6	27.4
Percentage of Israel's agricultural labor force (1963)	34.7	18.7
Percentage of Israel's Jewish agricultural labor force (1963)	44.5	24.0
Percentage of settlements' labor force engaged in agriculture (1963)	75.6	38.9
Percentage of settlements' labor force engaged in manufacturing, crafts, mining, and quarrying (1963)	4.9	20.1

Source: Statistical Abstract of Israel, 1964 and 1965. Government of Israel, Central Bureau of Statistics (Jerusalem, 1964, 1965).

THE KIBBUTZIM

Since this study is concerned mainly with the kibbutzim (collectives), only a brief mention is made of them here.

The 230 kibbutzim existing in 1964 had a population of 80,939 (including 190 non-Jewish residents). Fifty-nine per cent of these settlements (including 76 per cent of the total kibbutz population) had been established before Israel's independence.

This contrasts sharply with the development of the moshavim where 23 per cent of the settlements (with 22 per cent of the moshav population) date their existence to the pre-independence period. Again, unlike the moshavim, the agricultural economy of the collectives is diversified, and an increasing emphasis is placed on the non-agricultural enterprises. Between 1949 and 1962, the share of Israel's agricultural production provided by the collective settlements has varied, but has generally approximated 30 per cent of the total. In 1963 and 1964 the kibbutzim increased their agricultural production to a level approaching one-third of Israel's total.

PRIVATE JEWISH AND ARAB FARMS

Private agriculture (as distinct from the cooperative moshav and the collectives) consists of a large number of Jewish farms, most of which specialize in citriculture (mainly for export) and of Arab family farms. Although citrus production was but 14.6 per cent of the total value of agricultural production in 1964 (16.9 per cent when intermediate products are excluded), its importance to the Israeli economy is far greater; 14.2 per cent of Israel's commodity exports in 1964 consisted of citrus fruits; 8.1 per cent of commodity exports consisted of processed food-stuffs, most of which was derived from citrus. In terms of value-added (excluding the import content of exported goods) citrus played a much greater role, accounting for about 27 per cent of Israel's net earnings from commodity exports. About two-thirds of this important crop comes from the privately-owned citrus plantations. These are concentrated in the coastal area, where the land is, for the most part, privately owned. These plantations are managed along traditional principles of private enterprise and are largely dependent upon a hired labor force, provided by new immigrants in the neighboring towns and villages and temporary immigrant camps, as well as by the Arab sector. This contrasts sharply with both the collectives and the moshavim where the land is owned by the Jewish National Fund or the government and is leased to the settlements at nominal rentals, the basic capital being provided by the Jewish Agency on non-commercial terms, and many other forms of subsidization provided by the government and the Jewish Agency.

Israel's non-Jewish population — 11.3 per cent of the total

in 1964 — does not show the distinct trend towards urbanization typical of Israeli Jewry; 74.3 per cent of Israel's non-Jews (almost all Arab) lived in rural areas in 1964; among the Jews, 13.2 per cent. In the Jewish labor force, 10.6 per cent were engaged in agriculture; in the non-Jewish labor force, 39 per cent. Arabs provided 23.6 per cent of Israel's agricultural labor force (7.8 per cent of the total labor force). It is estimated that about half worked on their own family farms, the other half providing the seasonal and regular labor force requirements of other farms. These Arab farms accounted for 6.3 per cent of Israel's agricultural production in 1964. Arab agriculture is of greater importance than would be indicated by the above official data since a number of Jewish-owned farms are leased to Arabs for complete cultivation and harvesting or for the latter operation only. In certain crops such as olives, tobacco, sheep and goats, melons and certain vegetables, the Arab sector plays either a dominant or a very significant role.

In addition to these major agricultural sectors, namely, the moshav, the kibbutz, and private Jewish and Arab enterprises, the following minor sectors deserve brief mention.

Collective Moshavim. The first collective moshav was established in 1937, and by 1964 they were twenty-one in number with a population of 4,179. A collective moshav has a completely collectivized economy in the productive branches similar to the kibbutz, but unlike the latter, its consumption is organized along family lines. Women work in the collective productive branches in accordance with certain norms, determined mainly by the number and age of their children. The distribution of income is determined by the number of family dependents. Contrary to the expectations of many, this "cross" between the kibbutz and the moshav has failed to attract many adherents and has, in fact, declined both in terms of the number of settlements and population.

Schools. The agricultural sector also included (in 1964) nine agricultural schools with a population of 3,638.

Israeli agriculture is atypical in many respects. While other underdeveloped economies in the twentieth century have usually begun with an economy that is mostly agricultural, and have emphasized the reallocation of resources from agriculture to other sectors, the opposite was true in Israel where Jewish leadership stressed the development of agricultural settlements. In the pre-1948 era, the reasons for this policy were largely non-economic, viz., the political struggle with the British mandatory power which dictated the physical occupation of as large an area of Palestine as possible; internal security reasons; and the "ideological" conviction that the Jewish community in the developing Jewish homeland must not repeat the "abnormal" concentration of Jews in urban areas. In the initial period following independence, the strong emphasis upon agricultural settlement was strongly motivated by the necessity to provide for the mass of new immigrants, literally flowing into the country, and the importance of curtailing the importation of consumer goods so as to conserve foreign exchange for economic development.

Since the middle 1950's the problems facing Israeli agriculture have become similar to those that face the farmers in developed Western countries. The production of foodstuffs has increased to such a degree that the government and other public bodies have been compelled to come to the aid of the farmers (other than citrus) through direct subsidies, low-interest, long-term loans, production controls, and the sharp curtailment of the importation of foodstuffs. The motives for public aid were no longer to stimulate production, but rather to hold down the size of the farm surpluses, to compensate for the worsening parity index, and to reduce the gap between farm and non-farm incomes. The farm lobby is very effective in Israel.

Israel's natural conditions require a large investment in the development of new supplies of water for irrigation and the government and the other public bodies have invested considerable sums in the drilling of new wells, in irrigation networks, and more recently in the well-known plan to divert the waters of the Jordan River to the arid Negev. Water consumption in Israeli agriculture in 1964 was four times that in 1949. It has been estimated that only 5 per cent of Israel's potential water supply is found in the large southern provinces. In spite of government subsidies, certain areas, such as the Beisan Valley, enjoy considerable advantages as a result of the lower cost of their water supply.

In Table 2 the selected indicators of investment in agriculture and the value of agricultural production are indicative of the very high growth rates in this sector of Israel's economy. Between 1950 and 1964, production per worker in agriculture increased by 175 per cent, indicating an annual average rate of growth of 7.5 per cent.*

* A. L. Gaathon in his *Capital Stock: Employment and Output in Israel,*

TABLE 2. SELECTED INDICATORS IN ISRAELI AGRICULTURE
(1949 equals 100)

	1956	1962	1964
Value of agricultural production (corrected for price changes)	285	532	606
Per capita agricultural production	179	268	282
Total cultivated area	223	244	249
Irrigated area	322	472	488
Fruit plantations	151	219	235
Fish ponds	267	373	393
Tractors	363	688	831
Grain combines	183	210	196
Balers	199	297	339
Head of cattle (Jewish sector)	255	564	532
Laying hens (Jewish sector)	135	281	262
Sheep and goats (Jewish sector)	204	411	403
Water consumption in agriculture	409	446	404
Afforested area	419	655	743

Source: Annual Statistical Abstracts of Israel.

The effect of the sharp rise in agricultural production has been a strong downward pressure upon the prices of agricultural products, partially ameliorated by government subsidies. The consumer has been the beneficiary. Thus the rise in the over-all consumer price index between 1959 and 1964 was 33.9 per cent; the food component of the index rose 21.4 per cent. The prices of agricultural inputs increased by 30.8 per cent between 1959 and 1964, and the prices of outputs by 22.4 per cent.

The percentage of Israel's national income derived from agriculture which was 13.6 per cent in 1958 (based on net domestic product at factor cost) declined to 9.9 per cent in 1964 (compared with 25.4 per cent derived from manufacturing in 1964). This diminution was due to the greater expansion of manufacturing and other economic sectors, as well as the relatively unfavorable price movements in the agricultural sector. The variations in the agricultural sector are also partially a result of the periodic droughts of varying intensities. The disparity between per capita incomes in agriculture and those obtaining in the rest of the economy is generally smaller than that existing in the United

1950–1959 (Jerusalem, 1961) estimates (p. 32) that about two-fifths to one-half of the annual gross output or net product was due to increasing productivity (net of all inputs). In the latter half of the decade the contribution of productivity to the increase in output was about two-thirds.

States and in many other Western countries. In 1964 net incomes in agriculture were 70 per cent of the national average [4] (83 per cent in the Jewish sector [5]). However, subsidies to agriculture, both direct and indirect, have played an important part in the maintenance of farm incomes. Direct subsidies to farm owners accounted for 21 per cent of their net income in 1959; 29 per cent in 1960; 18 per cent in 1961, 22 per cent in 1962, and almost 25 per cent in 1963 and 1964. The sharp rise in 1960 was due to the serious drought which induced the government to provide the farmers affected with a larger than usual drought compensation. [6]

The composition of agricultural production has shifted over the years. The field crops are most susceptible to variations in rainfall. In 1964 they accounted for 18.3 per cent of the gross value of agricultural production.* However, within this broad category there has been a decided increase in the production of industrial crops, primarily, cotton, sugar beets, and peanuts. The relative position of the vegetable branches has been diminishing, reflecting, among other factors, their lower income elasticity. They accounted for 9.2 per cent of gross agricultural production in 1964. On the other hand citrus production has been of increasing importance, accounting for 14.6 per cent of the total; non-citrus fruits accounted for an additional 12.1 per cent. The rise in citrus production reflects the growing foreign demand for Israel's citrus crops; the growth of the non-citrus fruits reflects, in the main, the higher income elasticity of these products. Both the dairy and poultry branches have suffered from large surpluses in recent years. The production of cow's milk accounted for 8.9 per cent and eggs 10.2 per cent of Israel's gross agricultural production in 1964. In view of the heavy subsidization of these two branches the above figures would tend to exaggerate their position within the agricultural economy. The production of meat, chiefly poultry and beef, has shown the sharpest increase in recent years, accounting for 19.8 per cent of gross agricultural production in 1964. Fish production, primarily from the fish ponds of the kibbutzim, has suffered a relative decline as a result

* It is customary in Israel for agriculture to use the fiscal year, beginning October 1 and closing September 30, rather than the calendar year. Therefore the data given throughout this monograph in references to agriculture must be so understood. For example, data for agricultural production in 1959 refer to the last three months of 1958 and the first nine months of 1959.

of the decline in meat prices. In 1964, it accounted for 2.6 per cent of agricultural production.

Whereas per capita caloric intake has remained rather constant between 1954 and 1964 (2,830 calories in 1964), food consumption patterns have shifted markedly. Per capita consumption of meat has risen very sharply (more than quadrupled), a considerable rise has taken place in the consumption of fresh fruits, a small increase in egg consumption, and declines in the consumption of cereal products and fish. These trends reflect rising per capita incomes as well as relative price changes.

Annual gross investment in the farms was on a declining level between 1958 and 1963, although investment in tractors and other large agricultural equipment continued to increase (in 1964 investment in farms increased by 10 per cent). On the other hand, public development plans — especially the Jordan Irrigation Project absorbed increasing sums during this period. As in the previous years, the major sources of investment financing in agriculture were the government and the Jewish Agency and their subsidiaries (89 per cent in 1964 as compared with 74 per cent in 1958). In industry the share of public financing had declined from 42 per cent in 1958 to 9 per cent in 1964.[7] Significantly, since 1959, the sum total of new investment in the farms, financed from the farmer's own resources, was smaller than the real depreciation of farm assets.[8]

Israeli agriculture provides the population with the bulk of its food consumption, and the importation of food products (mainly wheat, vegetable oils, and animal feedstuffs) is offset by the export of food products (including processed foods). The development of industrial crops (such as cotton) and the increase in agricultural exports have enabled a further expansion of agriculture. However, the inexorable economic forces, which have brought about a relative decline of the farm sector in developed countries, have also been operative in Israel. Unless rising productivity can bring about much lower costs of production, enabling greater exports at international prices, a continued *relative* decline in the agricultural sector in Israel can be expected.*

---

* Data used in this and subsequent chapters, without mention of specific sources, are based upon the *Statistical Abstracts of Israel*, published annually in Jerusalem by the Central Bureau of Statistics of the Government of Israel.

II

HISTORICAL AND INSTITUTIONAL
BACKGROUND OF THE KIBBUTZIM

The large-scale anti-Semitic pogroms in Czarist Russia in the 1880's brought about a mass emigration of Jews from that country. Though most of them fled to the New World, a small number organized themselves in "Lovers of Zion" societies and emigrated to Palestine. The emergence of the World Zionist Organization in 1897 lent added stimulus and direction to this movement. By the turn of the century there were already a number of Jewish villages in Palestine, in addition to the more ancient urban Jewish communities. These villages consisted of privately-owned citrus plantations, situated along the coast, and some farms in the north, based upon cereal farming. The Jews who had come from Russia, fired with idealism but lacking in agricultural experience, were compelled to compete with primitive, poorly-paid Arab labor. This led to serious strife with the plantation owners and their overseers. In the meantime, the Zionist Organization developed a few large administered farms on tracts of land which it had purchased. Here, also, there was persistent strife between the farm administrators and their Jewish workers, and these farms frequently operated at a loss.

As a result of a strike which broke out on one of these administered farms at Kinnereth, in the Jordan Valley, the representatives of the Zionist Organization decided to lease a nearby tract of land to a group of workers for a year. The farm was to be collectively managed by them without any outside administrator. The conditions of the agreement were: a minimum wage plus 50 per cent of the net profits. These arrangements were of a provisional nature and gave the workers no claim to ownership of the farm. The financial success of this venture led to a more permanent arrangement, one which had been anticipated neither by the workers nor by the Zionist leaders. In fact, the latter considered the newly-expressed desire of the workers for a fully communal setup as antithetical to their concept of Jewish colonization and looked askance at the example set by this newly-founded colony, Deganiah. Even their final acquiescence was given in the conviction that "natural developments" would lead to the breakdown of the collective and to the development of small family-size farm units, with certain cooperative features.[1]

The kibbutz movement grew in spite of the upheavals of World War I, and by 1920 it numbered 40 collective groups with a total population of 650.[2] However, the Zionist leadership did not view this development favorably and espoused a different form of settlement called the moshav. Though certain agricultural workers' villages had been established before the war, the first moshavim, as they are now known, were established in the first few years after the war. The moshav was based upon individual family plots and family consumption. The charter of the moshav restricted the use of hired labor, provided for cooperative purchases and sales, and defined certain principles of mutual aid.

The fact that a considerable number of the members of Deganiah (the first kibbutz) left their collective to join moshav settlements encouraged the Zionist leadership in their belief that the "natural developments" they had predicted would lead to the transformation of the existing kibbutzim into moshavim. In fact, Chaim Weizmann, the leader of the Zionist movement (later to become the first president of the State of Israel), stated in 1920, "if we had the necessary funds, and if the conditions warranted it, we should begin the transformation of the kibbutzim into moshavim." [3]

The mushrooming of the number of kibbutzim to forty within a decade, each numbering between twenty and forty members, left most of them in a singularly weak financial and social position. The result was that only five kibbutzim of the forty existing in 1920 survived the decade, and even in these, few of the founding members remained.[4]

The period following World War I witnessed a general rise of Socialist sentiment in Europe. Most of world Jewry was concentrated in eastern Europe, and the resurgent anti-Semitism there helped to foster the growth of Zionism. While there were Jewish groups in these countries — primarily the Socialist "Bund" and the Jewish Communists — which felt that the solution of the "Jewish Problem" would inevitably follow the "victory" of Socialism, most Jews did not share this view. A number of Labor Zionist parties encouraged their youth to prepare themselves for emigration to Palestine for the realization of their Socialist ideals in the various kibbutz groups there, as a result of which many young Jews were attracted to these movements. Zionist organizations sent their representatives to European (and American) Jewish communities, where they formed youth groups and "preparatory farms" for those desiring to join the existing kibbutzim in Palestine or to establish new ones. Representatives of the kibbutzim in Palestine were sent to their affiliated youth organizations abroad, where they related the success of the collectives as pioneers of a new and better social order. The elimination of private property, the complete equality, the pure democracy, and the negation of exploitation excited the idealism of youth. The fructification of former swamp lands and desert soil gave their adherents a sense of "mission" in life. The opposition of the British Mandatory authorities and of the growing Arab Nationalist movement served to intensify the feeling of Jewish patriotism. But it was the rise of Hitlerism in the 1930's and its acceptance by many, even in the enlightened democracies, that tended to strengthen Jewish consciousness in many circles previously divorced from their Jewish heritage. The result was a considerable growth of the Zionist movement, including the pioneering kibbutz youth organizations.

Within the Jewish community of Palestine, the Histadrut supported the kibbutzim, although not to the exclusion of support for the moshavim. The leadership of the Zionist movement began to reconcile itself to the expressed desire of many pioneers for the collective form of settlement and to extend more active financial and other support. The reasons for this tardy acceptance of the kibbutz movement by the Zionist leadership were financial and political: (1) the initial investment necessary for a kibbutz was less than for a moshav, and the rearrangement of the existing kibbutzim into moshavim would have entailed considerable additional investment; (2) the increasing opposition of the British Mandatory authorities to expansion of Jewish settlement made it all the more urgent to expand Jewish colonization and to utilize the pioneering youth groups for that purpose; and (3) the increasingly active opposition of the Arab Nationalists brought defense considerations to the fore, and the kibbutz was more defensible than the moshav setup.

With the rise of anti-Semitism during the 1930's, the pressure of Jewish immigration to Palestine was constantly increasing. The large-scale Jewish immigration during the years 1933 to 1936 aggravated Arab-Jewish strife within the country itself and resulted in the British Mandatory government sharply curtailing the annual quota of Jewish immigrants permitted to enter Palestine. However, the arrangement between the government and the Jewish Agency was such that, although the former determined the immigration quotas, the latter allocated the visas. High priorities were given to young Zionists, trained in agriculture and in manual work, and educated in the use of Hebrew at the training farms.[5] These training farms, where the young pioneers were prepared for the rigors of future kibbutz settlement in outlying parts of Palestine, were increasing both in number and in membership throughout most of the European countries. In all these farms, operated by Zionist pioneering groups of varying political and religious affiliations, the sentiment in favor of collective settlement was paramount, and the communal structure was dominant in their organization.

As the persecution of Jews increased in Europe and the annual quota permitted by the British Mandatory authorities decreased (due to growing Arab Nationalist opposition), the waiting period for these pioneers also increased, and many of them had received several years of training before arriving in Palestine. The result was that a considerable percentage of Jewish immigrants during this period consisted of selected, well-trained adherents of the kibbutz movement. Furthermore, many of the new immigrants were so attracted by the security and social equality which the kibbutz offered that, in the period prior to 1948, the number of collectives grew more rapidly than the moshavim, and the kibbutz movement grew both absolutely and relatively. In 1931 there were 58 kibbutzim (including preparatory kibbutz groups) numbering 4,391 people and constituting about 2.5 per cent of the Jewish population in Palestine. By 1947, the kibbutz movement numbered 47,408 people, or 7.2 per cent of the Jewish population of the country.[6] In 1948, they reached what is generally considered the apex of their strength, in terms of the proportion of Jews in the country, members of kibbutzim, and in terms of their political, military, social, and economic influence. In that year, there were 149 collective settlements with a population of 54,200, constituting 7.9 per cent of the Jewish population and, significantly, 49 per cent of the Jewish rural population in the new State of Israel.[7]

The decade of the 1940's was the "golden age" of the kibbutz movement. The world war cut off most supplies from abroad, and the Allied armies in the Middle East provided a ready market for agricultural and industrial products at favorable prices, stimulating a vast expansion of agricultural and industrial production. Also, as early as the 1930's the kibbutzim had begun to develop light industry, and World War II gave a strong impetus to this development.

The kibbutzim constituted important centers for the Jewish underground forces which were organized by the leadership of the Yishuv (the Jewish community in Palestine), with the aid of the Zionist movement. They were the secret training centers for these forces, and kept their secret caches of arms. They also bore the major burden of the Zionist politically-motivated policy of settlement. In fact, a greater part of the Yishuv's general elite, in the political, military, and economic spheres, originated in the kibbutzim, and the latter preserved strong ties with these leaders.[8]

The struggle with the Mandatory government, which was relatively dormant during the war, was resumed as the war ended, due to the increasing pressure of Jewish refugees from Europe. In this struggle, the kibbutzim were in the vanguard, and again in the Arab-Jewish conflict of 1947-48 they were in the forefront. Though a few kibbutzim were destroyed during the conflict, the vast majority were successful in repulsing the Arab attacks, and the decisive contribution of the kibbutzim to the successful establishment of the State of Israel within its present borders is universally acknowledged.

THE KIBBUTZ MOVEMENT IN THE STATE OF ISRAEL

The successful establishment of the State of Israel in 1948 brought about a radically new situation. The Israeli government inherited large (in Israeli terms) tracts of land that had been the possession of the British Mandatory government and of the Arabs who fled the country. All restrictions on Jewish purchases of land and on immigration and colonization were removed. Many preparatory kibbutz groups in Israel which had previously been "land hungry" were quickly satiated, and kibbutz groups abroad which had been prevented from immigrating were now free to come to Israel and settle immediately. The pressures of security, which arose from the Arab-Jewish conflict, made the colonization and possession of outlying areas an urgent necessity. Thus by the end of 1949 the number of kibbutzim increased from 149 to 211, and the kibbutz population from 54,200 to 63,518. However, the large mass of immigrants coming to Israel during these years did not turn to the kibbutzim but, to the extent that they settled in the rural areas, turned mostly to the moshavim. The percentage of Jews in Israel living in kibbutzim has therefore been declining almost steadily from its high point of 7.9 per cent in 1948 to 3.6 per cent in 1964. Furthermore, in spite of the natural increase in the kibbutzim and some thousands of adherents from affiliated youth organizations in Israel and abroad who have joined them, the number of members who have left their kibbutzim has more than offset these sources of increase. According to the population survey of the Central Bureau of Statistics, the population of the kibbutzim in 1957 numbered 79,891, and then declined to 76,961 in 1961 (Appendix I). Between 1961 and 1964 the population increased to 80,749. Though the rural-urban movement of population is typical of developing and developed nations and though a similar trend is apparent in the largest rural sector in Israel (the moshavim), its social, economic, and political effects are much more pronounced in the kibbutz sector.

The fact that the mass immigration did not turn to the collectives created many problems for the kibbutzim. The need of the State to absorb the vast number of immigrants was of overwhelming importance. The Jewish population of Israel increased over 115 per cent in the four-year period following the declaration of independence! The new immigrants were, for the most part, lacking in capital and had to be provided with housing and jobs, and while the kibbutzim were anxious to admit them as candidates for membership, the ideological convictions of the kibbutz conflicted with the desire of the immigrants to be accepted as paid laborers. On the other hand, the large increase in population necessitated a regime of rationing of food supplies and other goods, and national policy demanded a greatly augmented scale of food production. The kibbutz movement, which had been the object of adulation of Jews in Israel and abroad, was now subjected to a torrent of criticism for being derelict in the performance of its national duties. On January 16, 1950, Prime Minister David Ben Gurion publicly denounced the kibbutz movement for its "shameful" policy of refusing to accept the new immigrants as hired laborers.[9] In fact, many kibbutzim had begun to use hired labor on a small scale even prior to Ben Gurion's denunciation, and economic and political pressures were instrumental in bringing about an increased use of paid workers. However, the official attitude of the movement was, and remains, that these are to be eliminated as quickly as possible.

Many duties which had been fulfilled by the collectives were now performed by the armed forces and by the general apparatus of the newly-founded State. Moreover, the kibbutzim had a considerable reservoir of trained manpower needed by the burgeoning governmental agencies, as well as by other public bodies (the Jewish Agency, the Histadrut, etc.), and many kibbutz members were attracted to these positions. It has been estimated that one-eighth of the *veteran* membership left their kibbutzim in the first five-year period after 1948.[10] Since the older members are frequently the skilled and managerial personnel, their departure was a serious loss to the collectives.

An additional blow which struck the kibbutz movement in the early 1950's was a result of internal political strife. The mounting difficulties of the State were reflected by increasing political tension throughout the country. The largest kibbutz federation, Hakibbutz Hameuhad, was literally torn asunder, and a few kibbutzim were actually subdivided into two separate settlements along political lines. In others there were "population exchanges" designed to maintain the political "purity" of each collective. This, too, caused the departure of a number of members from the kibbutz movement.

The kibbutz, being an "open" society in the sense that there are few restrictions on entry and none on leaving, has at *all* times had to face the problems attendant upon the departure of members, veterans as well as newer ones. However, until 1948, the number entering had generally exceeded the number leaving. The new situation which arose after Israeli independence changed this picture radically. Those kibbutzim which were well established before 1948 were able to cope with the new situation, but those founded more recently, especially most of the collectives which had begun after 1948, found themselves in an increasingly precarious position. These 100-odd kibbutzim (there were a total of 230 collectives in 1964) were "adopted" by the Settlement Department of the Jewish Agency. The economic activities of these settlements are now supervised, and they have in many respects lost their economic independence. The increasingly pressing financial difficulties of the "younger" kibbutzim (twelve antedate the State of Israel, most of the others were founded in 1948 and 1949), would surely have led to insolvency were it not for this "adoption" by the Jewish Agency. By 1957, 41 kibbutzim had become "directed settlements" and by 1962, a hundred were so listed. Furthermore, the government, the Jewish Agency, and the Workers' Bank (of the Histadrut) set up a fund of IL 600,000* for those kibbutzim which could not repay their debts (to private commercial banks and to suppliers).[11] This development constitutes a radical departure from the previous policy of the Settlement Department, namely, to provide land, water, and a settlement budget during the first few years and then permit the kibbutz to seek its own way. The substitution of low-cost, long-term loans for the high-cost, short-term debts, and provision of better planning and management have helped reduce or eliminate losses in these settlements.

INTERNAL ORGANIZATION

The kibbutz is divided into branches of production and consumption. The productive divisions include field crops, vegetables, fruit plantations, dairy, poultry, machine shop, carpentry, etc.; in many cases there are industrial units as well. Some kibbutzim (depending upon their location) have subdivisions dealing with fish ponds, or even deep sea fishing, apiculture, horticulture, sheep and goat raising. Many have building and construction divisions, though other kibbutzim, because of lack of manpower, skilled or unskilled, engage outside contractors for construction. The number and kind of productive branches depend upon the natural conditions obtaining in the area, the skills of its members, availability of capital, and upon the encouragement or discouragement of the governmental and Jewish Agency authorities in the form of credit rationing, allocation of imports, and over-all agricultural controls. The size of the labor force is an obvious limitation, so that the chronic labor shortage in the kibbutzim since the 1950's and the continued attempt to eliminate the hired laborers have brought about the curtailment or abolition of certain branches such as vegetable gardening.

* See Glossary, p. 168, for full discussion of the Israeli pound.

In the area of collective consumption there is a similar sub-division into kitchen and dining-room units (everyone eats in the communal dining hall, except for the younger children who usually have their own dining room); the laundry, a central clothing branch with its facilities for mending and ironing; the making of new clothing, shoe repairs (and in some cases the manufacture of new shoes); landscape gardening; children's homes, school facilities, etc. Each section, both of production and of consumption, is effectively directed in its daily operations by a manager appointed by the General Assembly or the Secretariat.

Legally, the supreme body of the kibbutz is the General Assembly, which elects the Secretariat, various functionaries, the committees, and sometimes the branch managers. These elections are generally held annually. The actual control of the kibbutz is in the hands of the Secretariat, which is the body held legally accountable by the State. The Secretariat usually numbers from five to seven members, consisting of a treasurer, external secretary (in many kibbutzim these two functions are frequently combined), internal secretary, economic manager, and one or two ex-officio members. The labor force manager is often included in the Secretariat.

Of the various committees elected annually by the General Assembly, the economic committee occupies an important place in the kibbutz hierarchy. It deals with over-all planning, efficiency of the various branches of production, and allocation of resources. The committee includes the economic manager as chairman, the labor force manager, frequently the treasurer, and the heads of the important production branches. The committee of personal services, usually headed by the internal secretary, includes the managers of the various consumption branches. In addition, there are committees on child welfare, school education, adult education, entertainment, and others. In effect, since the Secretariat controls the purse strings and the over-all labor force allocation, it restricts the scope of all the other committees.

In most kibbutzim, the number of members capable of undertaking managerial functions is very limited, so that there is a considerable amount of continuity, and hence, stability, in management. This would apply more to the older, well-established kibbutzim, which have achieved a much higher degree of internal stability, than to the younger settlements.

In the early days of the kibbutz movement, the egalitarian

ideas which were dominant seem to have dictated frequent changes in management so as to avoid the emergence of a permanent bureaucracy. This proved to be very costly, and the present arrangement is basically a compromise, with the greater emphasis on efficiency. The branch managers are changed quite infrequently, and often continue permanently in their positions. The over-all management is rotated among a small group every few years. It should be noted that managers may enjoy a certain amount of social prestige, but receive no additional economic benefits. On the contrary, these positions involve the acceptance of additional burdens and work beyond the normal eight- or nine-hour work-day, and are often shunned by the membership. These members must frequently be literally drafted for the job. This limited rotation of managerial personnel minimizes any loss of efficiency if any of them leaves the kibbutz or for other reasons becomes temporarily or permanently unavailable.

All able-bodied adults, men and women, must participate in the various tasks that the kibbutz requires. In the early years of the kibbutz movement, egalitarianism dictated that women participate in physically arduous tasks as well as in positions of responsibility. This was quickly abandoned, however, and today few women perform non-domestic jobs or those not common for women in Western societies. The sheer necessity for a large female staff in the domestic services, which increased with the rising number of children, created a relative shortage of women to fill these positions. The communal care of children might be considered by some to be superior but is, at the same time, more demanding from the viewpoint of man-hours or, rather, woman-hours.[12]

Besides furnishing managerial and office personnel for the various income-producing and consumption branches previously mentioned, many services, normally considered municipal functions, are provided in whole or in part by the collective. These would include water supply, sanitation, schools, and local defense. This wide range of non-income-producing work imposes considerable hardship upon the labor force organization. Wrangling and bickering between division heads for additional workers are a common occurrence and, notwithstanding the persuasive powers of the labor force manager, bitterness often results. In the private economy, differential wage-rates, as well as non-economic considerations, determine the allocation of labor. Although, in a general sense, income considerations are paramount in determining the allocation of labor in the kibbutz, this does not imply personal income, since no one in the collective is "paid" more than his fellow-members. The criterion of success of kibbutz management is primarily the profitability of its income-producing branches, which results in frequent claims of bias on the part of the consumption divisions in terms of the quantity and quality of the labor force assigned to them.[13]

In the early days of the kibbutz movement, members were frequently shifted from job to job, but the resulting inefficiency soon curtailed this practice. Today, almost every member has a certain skill (generally acquired through on-the-job training and/or formal training at the expense of the collective) and is almost always working in his chosen occupation. The "floating" labor force consists mainly of newcomers (generally unskilled); teen-age youth groups (Youth Aliyah) sent to the collectives by the Jewish Agency (provided with a half-day's schooling and a half-day's work); affiliated youth organizations (whose members choose to spend their vacations in kibbutzim); certain units (Nahal) of the army (who choose to spend most of their two and a half years of required national service in an agricultural settlement); and teen-age children of the members, who work part time, especially during school vacations.[14]

FEDERATIONS AND AFFILIATIONS

A description and analysis of the kibbutzim and their economy would be incomplete without a presentation of the various kibbutz federations and affiliations and of the economy and society in which they operate, particularly in the rural and agricultural sectors.

It is of particular importance to understand that the mere survival of many kibbutzim can be attributed to the direct and indirect power of these federations. The pattern and pace of development of all the collectives are strongly influenced by these federations. The considerable aid obtained by these organizations from the government, the Jewish Agency, and the Histadrut for their constituent collectives is of paramount importance. Though each individual kibbutz is organized along similar lines economically and socially, there are marked differences in political views and religious practices. These are the very *raison d'être* of six different federations.

Hakibbutz Ha'artzi, which has emerged as the strongest federation, is politically oriented to the left. Though it is non-Communist — it expels any member known to vote for the Communist party — it has a strong affinity with the goals of the world Communist revolutionary forces. It controls the Mapam political party. Though it provided but 18.7 per cent of its total vote in the elections to the Knesset (Israeli Parliament) in 1961, it retained a majority of the party's parliamentary seats for its kibbutz members. Hakibbutz Hameuhad, one of the three major kibbutz federations, might be described as a militant socialist group, neutralist in its attitude toward the major world blocs. It controls the Ahdut Ha'avodah political party. It, too, retained a majority of that party's parliamentary seats for kibbutz members in spite of the fact that this federation provided but 14.4 per cent of the party's total vote in the 1961 elections. The third major federation, Ihud Hakvutzot Vehakibbutzim, is affiliated with the Mapai party. This party, a Socialist party with a political platform similar to that of the British Labor party, has been the dominating force in the government of Israel since the inception of the State of Israel, as well as in the Histadrut and the Jewish Agency.* Unlike the other two major kibbutz federations, the Ihud does not control the political party with which it is affiliated. Nevertheless, its influence within the party goes far beyond the 3.2 per cent of that party's total vote, which the Ihud provided in the 1961 elections, the same being true of its parliamentary representation. Ha'oved Hatzioni Federation is affiliated with the centrist Liberty party; Hakibbutz Hadati, with the religious labor Hapoel Hamizrahi party; and the Po'alei Agudat Israel (religious) party has two kibbutzim affiliated with it. None of these smaller kibbutz federations has a controlling influence upon their respective political parties, though here, too, their influence is far greater than would be implied by their numerical strength.

The three largest federations comprised 92.4 per cent of the

---

* It has never attained an absolute majority in parliamentary elections, but through various coalitions has at all times retained the office of Prime Minister and the important portfolios in the government. The same is true of the dominant offices in the Jewish Agency, especially its control of the Settlement Department. In the Histadrut, it had an absolute majority (until September 1965).

total kibbutz population in 1964 (Appendix II). The authority of the federations in economic matters includes the distribution of manpower to their constituent settlements, the development of new settlements, the right to impose a "tax" on manpower, the granting of credit and many other activities.[15]

The distribution of manpower refers to the direction of new immigrants, pioneering youth groups in Israel and abroad, as well as any other individuals wishing to join one of the kibbutzim in their federation. Until the early 1950's, many were sent to found new settlements. The relative paucity of such youth groups during the last decade and the precarious position of most of the 100-odd "younger" kibbutzim has meant that these groups and individuals have been directed towards the reinforcement of existing collectives rather than the establishment of new ones. In many cases, the federations have directed the children of the older kibbutzim (those who, after returning from service in the armed forces, elect to remain in the kibbutz movement) towards the younger, weaker settlements of that federation.

The "tax" on manpower is the right of the kibbutz federation to demand that a certain percentage of the membership — usually 6 per cent — be released for various organizational activities outside their collectives. Older experienced managers from the established kibbutzim are sent to aid and direct the newer, less experienced settlements. Others are sent to affiliated youth organizations in Israel and abroad to attract additional recruits. Others direct the various federation activities and institutions, such as the collective loan funds, economic planning, purchasing, trucking and building cooperatives, educational institutions, and so on.

The kibbutz loan funds, which each federation maintains, provide emergency loans at low-interest rates to its member kibbutzim. These can often be crucial for the kibbutz. Furthermore, the loan funds can, by using their superior credit rating, receive loans from commercial sources not accessible to the weaker kibbutzim, and do so at lower interest rates. At other times, they will act as guarantors of loans made by commercial banks to their kibbutzim. In 1963, the accumulated reserves of these funds amounted to IL 22 million.[16]

All the kibbutzim (as well as most of the moshavim) market their produce through Tnuva, the large marketing cooperative of the Histadrut. Tnuva distributes about 70 per cent of the total agricultural produce of the country, and dominates the produce markets other than citrus fruits (mostly in the hands of private agriculture, not members of Tnuva). The industrial products of the kibbutzim are sold through Hamashbir, the large buying cooperative of the Histadrut, as well as through private channels. (Hamashbir serves the moshavim affiliated with the Histadrut, as well as other Histadrut institutions, and also maintains a number of large retail stores in the cities.) The kibbutzim do a large part of their purchasing at Hamashbir at wholesale prices.

All the collectives are members of Kuppat Holim, the Sick Fund or Health Insurance Plan of the Histadrut. Kuppat Holim owns and maintains clinics and hospitals throughout the country, providing medical services and drugs to its dues-paying members. The majority of the population of Israel belongs to Kuppat Holim.

The Histadrut-affiliated Audit Union for kibbutzim and most moshavim has aided in the standardization of accounting and office management procedures. Generally speaking, commercial banks will not deal with a collective unless it receives its annual balance sheet and profit and loss statement as approved by the Audit Union. The economic data compiled by the Audit Union are of inestimable help in economic management and for comparative analysis of various collectives as well as of the kibbutz movement as a whole.

Other Histadrut institutions of importance to the kibbutzim are the large Workers' Bank, various credit unions, Mekorot (a water company owned jointly with the government and the Jewish Agency, which drills wells and maintains a network of pipes throughout the country), and the Agricultural Center with its considerable influence in governmental and Jewish Agency departments.

The kibbutzim actively participate in and dominate many of the regional councils, equivalent to the county organizations in the United States. A number of these regional councils have set up large industrial establishments, owned and operated by the councils, for the manufacture of animal fodder and other products.

The kibbutz has, of course, many dealings with various governmental departments, primarily the Ministry of Agriculture. The increasing industrialization of the collectives has necessitated frequent dealings with the Ministry of Commerce for the allocation of imported raw materials, loans from the Development Budget, etc.

Since its very early years, the kibbutz movement has maintained a close relationship with the Jewish Agency, primarily its Settlement Department. Through the Jewish National Fund (associated with the Jewish Agency through the World Zionist Organization), the collectives (and most moshavim) are provided with land on a 49-year (renewable) lease basis, at a very low annual rental, payable after the settlement is considered well established. Even this nominal rental is frequently suspended or deferred in hardship situations, such as drought. Through the Settlement Department, the settlements are provided with very long-term loans at low interest rates which the settlement begins to repay after it is considered self-supporting. As has been noted earlier, the Jewish Agency has more recently gone much further by undertaking financial responsibility for many younger kibbutzim in existence for fifteen or twenty years, who might otherwise have suffered bankruptcy. However, quite frequently, due to the financial difficulties of the Jewish Agency, there have been lengthy delays between the approval of a budget and its actual grant to the settlement, causing extreme hardship to the kibbutzim.

All these affiliations of the kibbutzim have been of immeasurable aid in their establishment and development, and an understanding of these institutional arrangements is essential for a comprehensive analysis of their economy.

III

OPERATION OF THE KIBBUTZ ECONOMY

Under a system of private enterprise, economists theorize that though the entrepreneur "could have and historically has had, very diverse goals, to be his own boss, to maintain a customary standard of living, to obtain money and economic power, to obtain political power, etc., . . . it is customary to attribute to him one overriding goal: the maximization of profits. . . . Profit maximization is the strongest, the most universal, and the most persistent of forces governing entrepreneurial behavior. This is a judgment based upon wide observation . . . and especially, from the success of predictions based on this assumption." [1]

FACTORS OF PRODUCTION AND THEIR ALLOCATION

The history of the kibbutz movement, the ideology of the collective, and wide observation of its economy, indicate that an analysis based on these assumptions would not be applicable to the kibbutz as a producing unit. The settlement of so many kibbutzim in areas of inadequate rainfall, poor prospects for well water, inferior soil, malaria-infested swamps, great distances from and poor communication with the market, dangerous security conditions, and difficult climatic conditions cannot be reconciled with a theory of enterprise which assumes profit maximization. The kibbutzim were motivated by the fulfillment of Jewish national goals rather than by private profit. The abolition of private property and the distribution of income according to the Socialist tenet "from each according to his ability and to each according to his needs" are antithetical to the concept of profit maximization.

The economic criteria of the kibbutz were never predetermined; they evolved as a result of constant and persistent efforts to increase and to expand within the limits of possibility. The

kibbutz movement never ruled out the desirability of profits or of capital accumulation as a result of saving. Although it has usually placed what it considered its duties above the drive for profits, it has always striven to attain a self-supporting economy as quickly as possible, so that a deficit was at all times considered by its members to be a social as well as an economic calamity.[2]
- The goals of the kibbutz economy have been defined as: "a) colonization of the land; b) increasing production, especially agricultural production; c) expansion of the agricultural population; and d) attainment of a 'decent' standard of living for the members." [3] Within the constraints of quantity and quality of land, water, capital, and human resources, the kibbutz has striven to maximize production, especially agricultural production. With the price of their products determined by the government and/or market forces, the collectives have exerted their efforts towards acquiring a maximum of capital resources. These acquisitions, however, have frequently had the effect of diminishing their net profitability (see Chapter V). The evidence is also quite clear that other sectors of Israeli agriculture have much more readily shifted their resources towards those branches in agriculture which became more profitable.

In reality, since the middle 1950's (at least), the kibbutzim have suffered frequent losses, and even many of the older established kibbutzim have found it difficult to balance their budgets and to meet their obligations. The result has been that economic pressures have made the kibbutz much more profit-conscious. Certainly the increasing role of non-agricultural enterprises (contrary to the ideological belief in the primacy of agriculture) can be ascribed to this factor. One can detect a sense of pride in the boasts of certain members that their branch earns a higher "yom avodah" (net income per work-day) than do the other branches of the economy.

Before 1948, the Zionist and Socialist ideals were basic to the motivation of the kibbutz members; since then, the nationalist fervor has cooled considerably. It might very well be significant that of the three major kibbutz federations, the one with the strongest Marxist convictions has emerged as the strongest federation and has gained in population in recent years (although very slightly) while the others have lost.

Land. The Jewish National Fund, which was organized by the World Zionist Organization in the early part of this century was of paramount importance in the Jewish agricultural settlement of Palestine, and was of crucial importance to the organization of kibbutzim and moshavim. The principles of the Jewish National Fund involved, basically, the purchase of land in Palestine (and later in Israel) which was to remain under its inalienable ownership and to be rented on the basis of 49-year renewable leases to those undertaking to cultivate the land on their own. Although the latter principle is not strictly enforced — both kibbutzim and moshavim have been using hired labor — the fact remains that the land is allocated in such units as will lend themselves to cultivation by the lessee and his family, or by the collective as a whole. This arrangement succeeded in preventing the growth of a Ricardian land-owning class earning a growing share of the national product, or at least of the agricultural product, as "economic rent." Similarly, it prevented the continual fragmentation of the farm units such as occurred in a number of European and Middle Eastern countries.

In 1947, the Jewish National Fund owned 53.8 per cent of all the land owned by Jews in the country. Another 25.1 per cent was owned by a foundation set up in the latter part of the nineteenth century by a Jewish philanthropist, Baron Edmond de Rothschild, for the purpose of encouraging Jewish agricultural settlement. This organization also adopted colonization principles quite similar to those of the Jewish National Fund. Private Jewish land ownership, 21.1 per cent of the total, was concentrated mostly in the urban areas and in private citrus plantations.[4]

After the Mandatory government restrictions were removed in 1948, the Jewish National Fund expanded its landholdings considerably, so that today it owns most of the cultivated area of Israel. Over 600 settlements, about one-fourth of the Jewish population (and the large majority of the Jewish rural population) are settled on its land. About 90 per cent of the land of Israel is owned either by the State or the Jewish National Fund.

It has been estimated that those who lease their land from the public landowners pay a rental which averages less than 0.4 per cent of the gross value of the agricultural output. However, "while rent is a trivial item of expenditure, the situation of the land in relation to the sources of irrigation water, and its distance to the nearest urban market, is of such significance that the arbitrary decision of Jewish Agency officials where a new settlement should be located, is of paramount importance, and may be the source of windfall profits for the lucky group." [5] A brief look at a map of Israel would readily show that the large majority of kibbutzim are not members of this "lucky group." This was initially the choice of the collectives who put national duty before personal profit, but having made that choice, it has a permanent effect upon their viability.

Until 1948, the kibbutzim had much less land than they were able to cultivate profitably. In 1929 they had 70.3 dunams per family (one dunam is approximately one-quarter of an acre), but the pressure of Jewish immigration in the 1930's and 1940's and the increasing land restrictions of the Mandatory government drastically reduced this land quota, so that by 1947 the cultivated land per family was only 30.9 dunams. Partly offsetting this was the growth of the irrigated area from a negligible quantity in 1929 to 6.8 dunams per family in 1947.

In 1948, vast new areas became available, including lands abandoned by the Arabs and State-owned lands taken over by the new Jewish government. The government turned to the kibbutzim to cultivate these lands, since they had the equipment and the "know-how." The collectives greatly increased their landholdings, both those allocated to them on a permanent basis and those leased to them on a short-term temporary basis. Between 1947 and 1952 landholdings per family in the kibbutz almost tripled to 88 dunams. As the new immigrants who generally settled in moshavim acquired agricultural experience, they demanded and received much of the land which had been allocated to the kibbutzim on a temporary basis. By 1959, the allotment per kibbutz family unit had been reduced to 74 dunams, and 73 dunams in 1963.[6]

The climatic and topographical conditions in Israel make the problem of irrigated land one of major importance. In addition to the very heavy capital investment in land in the form of farm buildings, fences, drainage, roads, and fertilization, there is a very large investment in irrigation. Israel is a subtropical country with a widely varied topography. The quantity of rainfall varies considerably not only from north to south, but also in accordance with the elevation of the area. Some areas, which receive adequate average rainfall, have considerable variation from year to year. Even though the total rainfall is sufficient in a certain year, its "timing" may be poor, so that if too long a time elapses between the fall sowing and the first rains, the crops suffer considerable or irreparable damage. With irrigation, many crops which would otherwise be impractical have been introduced; the land is more fully exploited during the dry summer months; yields are often increased as much as five-fold; land and labor are conserved through the raising of large crops on smaller areas; two, and sometimes three, crops are raised during a year, each with a much higher yield than the single, non-irrigated crop; and the uncertainties of non-irrigated agriculture are minimized. Furthermore, part of the southern area of Israel, the Negev, previously uncultivable because of its very light rainfall, has become productive through irrigation.

Public water projects in Israel are on a very large scale. The Mekorot Water Company (owned by the government, the Jewish Agency, and the Histadrut) provided for the transfer of water from the north and center of Israel to the arid south, utilizing the firm flow of rivers, the unutilized groundwater, and the spring flow surpluses. The large-scale Jordan water scheme, being currently completed, aims at transferring the headwaters of the Jordan River from the extreme north to the south in 108-inch pipes.[7]

Supplementing the public irrigation schemes, the farms have invested large sums (through public loans) in expanding their irrigated area. While the cultivated area of the kibbutzim has been almost constant since the early 1950's, their irrigated area has increased very greatly. In 1952, only 9.5 per cent of the cultivated area in the collectives was irrigated. By 1955, the percentage had increased to 19.8, in 1959 it had reached 30 per cent of their cultivated area, and 35 per cent in 1962.[8]

The allocation of their land and water resources has varied over time. The agricultural policy of the kibbutzim is based on their belief in diversified agriculture, in contradistinction with most older moshavim which have become dairy and/or poultry farms. Private Jewish agriculture, as well as that in some of the moshavim, is almost exclusively devoted to citrus plantations. However, within the policy of diversification in the kibbutzim there have been considerable changes in the ratio of the "mix," and the location of the settlement becomes a decisive factor in determining the allocation of the land and water resources. Government encouragement or discouragement in the forms of subsidies, credits, and other forms of aid designed to stimulate, or controls designed to limit production, have certainly affected the allocation of these resources in the kibbutzim.

The land devoted to field crops has diminished both relatively and absolutely. In 1950, the collective settlements allocated 88.6 per cent of their cultivated area to field crops, including wheat, barley, and fodder. In 1959 72.4 per cent was cultivated with field crops, and 77.6 per cent in 1963. Within the broad area of field crops, industrial crops have become increasingly important, primarily sugar beets, cotton, peanuts, sunflowers, flax fibre, and safflower. In 1955, they allocated somewhat over 1 per cent of their land to these crops. By 1959 it approximated 3.6 per cent of their cultivated area, and reached 9.0 per cent in 1963. Between 1959 and 1961 the area of industrial crops increased 141 per cent. The relatively large areas available to the kibbutzim and the high degree of mechanization in the cultivation of these crops make them uniquely suitable for the collectives.

On the other hand, the kibbutzim have tended to relinquish vegetable production to the moshavim. In spite of the very large increase in irrigated area, in 1950 they had allocated 23,410 dunams to the raising of vegetable crops, or 2.3 per cent of their total cultivated area. By 1952, they had increased this area to 31,851 dunams, though the proportion of the total cultivated remained constant. In 1959, the area allocated by collectives to vegetables had decreased to 29,193 dunams, and by 1963 the area had been further reduced to 27,514 dunams. There are a number of reasons for this, primarily the appearance of surpluses in vegetables since the middle 1950's and the fact that, with the presently known technology, most vegetable production does not lend itself to large-scale mechanization and therefore necessitates a large seasonal labor force. Because of the increasingly strong opposition of the kibbutzim to the use of hired labor, they have gradually reduced the growing of vegetables.

Fruit plantations have become increasingly important in the collectives. Between 1947 and 1950, their area increased from 22,000 to 47,000 dunams, and by 1959, it had reached 110,000 dunams, of which 103,000 dunams were irrigated. Of this area, 30 per cent was citrus, 14 per cent vineyards, 17 per cent bananas, 19 per cent apples, pears, and plums, and the other 20 per cent in olives, carobs, and various subtropical fruits. The large increase in fruit plantations has brought about surpluses of many fruits (other than citrus, which goes mostly into the export market). The continual profitability of citrus has induced the collectives to concentrate increasingly on that branch. However, the bulk of their citrus plantations had not yet reached the fruit-bearing age by the end of 1959. Banana plantations are located mainly in the hot climate of the Jordan Valley, and the collectives there effectively monopolize this market. In 1963 the area of fruit plantations in the kibbutzim was 142,000 dunams.

Fish ponds are another area where the kibbutzim enjoy an almost complete monopoly. In 1950, 21,093 dunams were allocated to this branch, and by 1959 it had almost doubled, to 41,358 dunams, and reached 51,499 dunams in 1963. They are to be found mostly in the northern part of the country where the water supply is relatively plentiful and inexpensive.[9]

Labor. It is the opinion of observers today that in addition to the underlying (attenuated) ideological convictions of the kibbutz member, the economic security afforded by the kibbutz is a strong motivating force. So long as he remains in the kibbutz he will not face the problems of unemployment, seasonal or cyclical. No personal misfortune will affect the economic well-being of his family, and the kibbutz will provide for his old age. True, such motivation exists in all societies. Job security, old age pensions, and other forms of economic security will induce many to accept, say, civil service positions in the United States in preference to higher-paying private employment. However, the economic security of the kibbutz far transcends in scope that obtaining in civil service or in similar positions. It would seem that, today, this is the overriding motive and incentive of many kibbutz members.[10]

While in all societies, including the Soviet, differential wage-rates and other economic rewards provide the incentive for greater productive effort, this incentive is present only in a very limited and indirect manner in the case of the kibbutz member. While the member will not be individually rewarded with any economic benefits for greater effort, he is aware that the greater economic success of the kibbutz will have an indirect positive effect on his personal economic welfare.

There are non-economic motives, however, which are quite potent. In a small social unit personal recognition on the part of the group is a strong motivating factor. Recognition of the individual by the society as a good, devoted and successful worker is more than the equivalent of a "Good Citizenship Award," because of the strong social pressures generated by a small, closely-knit society. Conversely, social opprobrium, the fate of one looked upon as a "slacker," can, without any formal act of the kibbutz, cause that member to leave the collective.[11]

The kibbutz member (usually a newer one) so long as he is unskilled and therefore a "cork" in the labor force, plugging up any manpower gaps in the various branches, is frequently shifted from one type of work to another, and is looked down upon by the membership. He has a strong incentive to acquire some special skill, either through on-the-job training or by being sent to one of the courses organized by the kibbutz federation or by one of the national organizations, or a combination of both. Once skilled, he is identified with one of the income-producing branches and develops a greater sense of stability and "ownership." The more skilled and more ambitious members become heads of branches or even over-all managers who are highly "rated" by their fellow members. These incentives are stronger in kibbutz society because of the absence of differential wage-rates.[12]

In the kibbutz the division of labor between the income-producing branches and the service branches is dependent largely upon the ratio of children to adults. To a certain extent, this is true of the urban or moshav family unit as well. However, while in the moshav the mother would be helping with the chickens and performing other "chores" — even with a number of younger children at home — in the kibbutz the care of three children would involve at least a full work-day of an adult. The average number of work-days per child (i.e., under three years of age) is 120 days per year. Since exclusive of Sabbaths, holidays, sickness, annual vacation, etc., the kibbutz member works an average of 265 days per year, the services of one adult member would provide the needs of somewhat more than two children in this age group. In the four- to seven-year age group, the number of work-days per child is approximately 80, including kindergarten and teaching staff. Here one adult member would serve more than three children. Thus the birthrate has a direct and marked bearing upon the division of labor in the kibbutz, between the income-producing and non-income-producing branches, due to the institutional patterns of the consumption branches, particularly in child care.[13]

In their early formative years, the collectives sent most of their labor force to work for private farmers or in nearby industries. Most of their income was from outside employment as hired laborers. The income was, of course, pooled, as is any income acquired by a kibbutz member. As they received land and a settlement

budget from the Jewish Agency, they gradually reduced the
number of persons working elsewhere and employed them in
their own economy. The strong drive of the kibbutzim to invest
heavily and expand production, coupled with the sharp diminution in the number joining the movement since the early 1950's,
has turned the labor surplus prevalent in the kibbutzim until the
1940's into the acute labor shortage typifying the collective movement since the independence of Israel. Though there are still
kibbutz members working elsewhere, these are usually people
in important positions in the government, Jewish Agency, or
Histadrut, trucking cooperatives, and other ventures in which
the kibbutz has an interest. Since they are generally in the upper
echelons, the cash income which the kibbutz derives is not in-
considerable, and, even more important, the influence of these
people makes it worthwhile for the kibbutz movement to maintain these positions, the severe manpower shortage in the kibbutzim
notwithstanding. In addition, the kibbutzim rent their agricultural machinery to other settlements (along with their operators)
so as to utilize more fully the heavy investments in machinery
made by the kibbutzim.

Since Hakibbutz Hameuhad constituted 28.9 per cent of the
kibbutz movement in 1958, one can assume that the distribution
shown in Table 3 is quite typical of the movement as a whole.
However, these averages conceal considerable differences between
one kibbutz and another. Generally speaking, the older settlements have a higher ratio of labor-days in manufacturing. In a
few, one can find a ratio of industry to agriculture as high as two
to one in favor of the former. Another important distinction
between the older and younger settlements is in the percentage

TABLE 3. ALLOCATION OF LABOR-DAYS IN HAKIBBUTZ HAMEUHAD IN 1958
(in percentages)

INCOME-PRODUCING	PER-CENTAGE	NON-INCOME-PRODUCING	PER-CENTAGE
Agriculture	24.5	Services for adults	15.1
Manufacturing and crafts	10.8	Services for children	19.5
Outside work	6.1	Courses and federation activities	5.0
Construction and other investment	2.1	Vacations, illness, maternity, military reserve duty, etc.	11.3
Administration, storage, etc.	5.6		
Percentage of labor-days in income-producing work	49.1	Percentage of labor-days not income-producing	50.9

Source: *Statistical Manual* of Hakibbutz Hameuhad (October 1959), p. 4.

of labor-days in administrative work and other general services. The younger kibbutzim are generally underpopulated, necessitating a burdensome "overhead" in terms of various services which could well serve a larger membership. Economies of scale are as applicable to the service branches as to the income-producing branches. Since 1954 the Central Bureau of Statistics of the government has been conducting labor force surveys using sampling methods; and since 1958 these surveys have been conducted four times a year, thus making it possible to calculate an average distribution of the labor force (Table 4).

TABLE 4. DISTRIBUTION OF LABOR FORCE IN KIBBUTZIM BY ECONOMIC BRANCH

	1958	1959	1960	1961	1962	1963
Number of kibbutz members in labor force in Israel	55,700	51,900	51,000	43,300	44,500	52,200
Labor force employed in kibbutzim	56,700	55,000	54,600	46,800	46,300	55,800

Percentage Distribution of Labor Force Employed in Kibbutzim

	1958	1959	1960	1961	1962	1963
Agriculture	37.7	37.1	38.8	38.0	38.9	38.9
Manufacturing and crafts	20.8	19.6	18.6	19.3	18.1	20.1
Construction and public works	1.8	1.4	1.6	1.7	1.6	1.4
Electricity, gas, water, and sanitation	1.7	1.3	1.0	0.7	0.1	0.4
Commerce and banking		0.2	0.6	0.3	0.1	0.3
Transport, storage, and communications	3.9	4.4	3.1	2.9	4.0	2.6
Government, public and business services	11.6	15.3	15.7	15.1	14.2	15.2
Personal services and recreation	22.5	20.7	20.6	22.0	23.0	21.1

Source: Statistical Abstracts of Israel.

The fact that the kibbutz records refer to labor-days, and the governmental figures to labor force, the two sets of data will not necessarily correspond. For example, those temporarily ill, on maternity leave, or on reserve duty will be recorded by the Central

Bureau of Statistics as employed in their usual occupations; when labor-days are recorded, they will be included in the non-income-producing tabulation. One must also consider the possibility of sampling errors in the government survey.

Capital. Of the three traditional factors of production, the role of capital has been the only consistent one in the economy of the kibbutzim, in the sense that it was at all times a limiting factor in their development. Before the establishment of the State of Israel, labor was relatively plentiful, with a considerable proportion of the members dependent upon employment outside the kibbutz economy. Since 1948, and increasingly since the mid-1950's labor has become very scarce, as is evidenced by kibbutzim hiring laborers contrary to their avowed principles. In the case of land, the record is the reverse of that of labor. Before 1948, the increasingly severe restrictions upon Jewish land purchases imposed by the British Mandatory government on the one hand and the increasing pressure towards immigration and colonization on the other made for an increasing scarcity of land. Since 1948, there has been a radical change in Israel, with a shortage of settlers rather than of available land for settlement.

Kibbutzim (as well as most moshavim) started out without any capital of their own. The Jewish Agency which derived its funds from contributions of world Jewry provided the basic investment capital. Until 1930 all the expenditures of the settlement department of the Jewish Agency were in the form of grants. In 1930, agreements were made with the Jewish Agency providing for 50-year loans at 2 per cent. Generally, such agreements were signed when the settlement was considered "established," usually five or ten years after the initial act of settlement. In the mid-1930's the agreements provided for 25-year loans at 4 per cent. In 1948-49 the terms were for 25 or 30 years at 3 per cent. More recent loan agreements were for 30-year periods at 3.5 per cent. It should be emphasized that these are non-commercial loans in every sense of the word, and are frequently deferred in difficult times. The interest rate is much lower than the 10 per cent rate, or higher, prevalent in commercial banks in Israel.[14]

The pressing needs of the Jewish Agency restricted its ability to provide the settlements with all their needed investment funds, and even the budget allocated to the kibbutzim was often provided after lengthy delays. The result was an increasing dependence upon private credit. At first, the commercial banks were wary of dealing with these "utopian" societies, whose stability was widely questioned. Even as late as 1929, twenty years after the establishment of the first kibbutz, the total of all private bank loans to the collectives was about 11 per cent of their total debt. Within the next decade a radical change took place with respect to the attitude of private capital towards the collectives. By 1937, commercial loans to the kibbutzim had increased more than ten-fold, reaching 38 per cent of their total debt. The much higher percentage is due not only to the greater willingness of private capital to finance kibbutz development, but also to the fact that the older kibbutzim of that time were considered going concerns, no longer entitled to loans from the Settlement Department.[15]

In addition to the Settlement Department budgets and private commercial loans, there are several other sources of capital available to the kibbutzim. The Histadrut maintains a number of financial institutions, the largest of which is the "Workers' Bank." This functions by the same principles as private commercial banks but is subject to the general policy of the Histadrut to provide capital for "productive" purposes, primarily to those affiliated with the Histadrut. The latter's large insurance company and the various savings and loan associations and welfare funds are also important sources of capital. Since the founding of the State of Israel, the government has maintained a separate "Development Budget" providing long-term, low-interest loans to agriculture and industry. The agricultural loans are channeled through the "Israel Bank of Agriculture," a semi-autonomous governmental institution providing the bulk of the long-term, and most of the intermediate-term, credit to Israeli agriculture. Generally, they restrict their loans to those settlements that are considered well established and therefore no longer subject to the patronage of the Jewish Agency.

The combined effect of the strong drive within the kibbutzim to expand their productive facilities and the capital they mobilized from the various sources is illustrated in Table 5. Obviously the list is incomplete, but the trend indicated is unmistakable. In the period before 1947, primarily the prior decade, the pace of investment was approximately in keeping with the large growth in the number of kibbutzim and their membership. Considering the impediments — the Second World War, the growing hostility of the Mandatory government, and the increasing defense burdens

TABLE 5. SELECTED INDICATORS OF INVESTMENT IN AGRICULTURE
IN THE ECONOMY OF THE KIBBUTZIM (1947 = 100)

	1952	1956	1959	1963
Labor force (employed in agriculture)	151	166	172	174
Cultivated area (unirrigated)	479	417	376	333
Irrigated area	180	407	576	663
Fruit plantations	253	378	498	643
Tractors	577	801	910	1,041
Combines (grain)	327	307	361	300
Balers	280	337	358	296
Trucks and other motor vehicles [a]	268	325	337	398
Poultry (laying hens and chickens) [b]	377	522	653	565
Cattle (dairy and beef)	203	251	427	535
Sheep and goats	191	249	235	215
Work animals	64	56	48	44
Fish ponds	295	347	373	464

Sources: I. Shatil, *The Economy of the Communal Settlements in Israel: Principles and History* (Tel Aviv, 1955), pp. 376–377. The Audit Union for Cooperative Agriculture, *Statistical Manuals of the Kibbutzim* (Tel Aviv, March 1957 and April 1960), pp. 2–18.

[a] The decline in the number of trucks between 1959 and 1963 was offset by a greater increase in the number of smaller vehicles. Thus, it may very well be that the total investment in motor vehicles actually declined.
[b] The decline between 1959 and 1963 was probably offset by increased investment in poultry for meat and in the production of eggs for hatcheries.

accompanying Arab hostility — this was a notable achievement. Between 1947 and 1952, when a large increase took place in the number of collectives and their members, the tempo of investment was far greater. Since 1952, and especially since 1956, kibbutz membership has increased very little, but investment continues to add to the productive capacity per worker in the collectives. The non-irrigated cultivated area continues to decrease because of the large expansion of the irrigated area. The number of work animals has declined because of increasing mechanization. The number of trucks and other vehicles owned directly by the settlements has risen moderately since 1956 on account of the increasing trend towards regional trucking cooperatives, jointly owned and operated by the settlements. These cooperatives are incorporated separately, and their assets do not appear directly on the balance sheets of the kibbutzim other than the value of their shares.

Figures for 1956 show that the kibbutzim allocated almost 30 per cent to housing, communal buildings, and durable consumer goods, the rest to buildings, equipment, and irrigation installations in order to expand their agricultural and industrial productive capacity.[16]

A study of 113 established kibbutzim (almost all set up before 1948, and containing most of the total population) indicates that for the period 1955 to 1959, inclusive, fixed assets increased a nominal 114 per cent.[17] Since the investment price index rose during the five-year period by about 20 per cent and since the population changed very slightly, this would indicate an additional real investment per worker in the order of 90 to 95 per cent.

Generally, the younger kibbutzim channel a larger percentage of their total investment towards expansion of productive capacity. They will usually get along for a number of years in simple wooden frame houses and similar buildings for the communal dining hall and kitchen, though they will insist, at the very outset, on the best facilities for the children.

An estimate published in 1960 indicated that investment in manufacturing and crafts in the collectives was about one-third of that in agriculture (see Table 6).[18] With the increasing agricultural surpluses and consequent governmental encouragement of industrial expansion, one can expect this percentage to increase.

TABLE 6. VALUE OF AGRICULTURAL PRODUCTION IN 1960
(in thousands of Israeli pounds)

PRODUCT	ISRAEL	KIBBUTZIM	KIBBUTZ % OF TOTAL
Field crops	126,115	48,736	38.6
Vegetables	60,632	11,954	19.7
Citrus fruits	108,637	8,700	8.0
Other fruits	78,783	35,307	44.8
Cow's milk	72,394	19,896	27.5
Beef	53,799	16,875	31.4
Eggs	93,712	25,102	26.8
Poultry meat	71,825	29,139	40.6
Fish	18,749	9,958	53.1
Honey	2,009	608	30.3
Miscellaneous (including increased value of livestock, fruit plantations, etc.)	62,212	28,048	45.1
Total value of gross agricultural product	748,867	234,323	31.3

Sources: Statistical Abstract of Israel, 1961. Economic Quarterly (March 1962), p. 102.

FINANCES

Any large-scale enterprise must conduct itself in accordance with accepted accounting principles, with as much speed and accuracy as possible. Since the collective is a unit of consumption as well as of production, this dictum would be even more applicable to the kibbutz. The complexity of the collective organization; its many production and consumption branches; the assets of the collective; the concern for the personal welfare of its members; the collective aspects of child rearing and education; the social and cultural character of the membership; the planning of the economy and the efficiency of its execution; the organization of the consumption branches; purchase and sales; investment and its financing; municipal functions, such as the provision of schools, water, electricity, sanitation, local defense; its participation in the political, social, and economic life of the country; all these are reflected in the kibbutz accounts. These accounts mirror all the activities of the kibbutz and provide the means of checking upon and improving its performance.[19]

The kibbutz keeps a separate account of the expenditures in money and in kind for the upkeep of adults, children, aged parents of the members, Youth Aliyah groups, Nahal military units, and so on. The accounts provide for a proportional allocation of services for consumption, such as water and electricity, and for production as in irrigation, machine shop, manufacturing, etc.; they list any internal provisions of supplies such as vegetables, poultry, meat, and dairy products (but at a lower price than the one the kibbutz would obtain from the sale of these products, since there are no costs of transportation and other selling costs); they allow for depreciation of inventory and equipment in the consumption branches and of the houses, kitchen and dining hall, children's homes, and so on; they record any financial expenditures (not repaid) for outside political activity on behalf of the political party, kibbutz federation, or the Histadrut; and they record the "pocket money" given to members for vacations and other minor expenses. However, the money equivalent of the workdays in the consumption branches is not included on the theory that this is analogous to the work which the housewife would do in her private home.

All labor-days are recorded, both in the income-producing and in the service branches. Insofar as able-bodied adults are concerned, each day's work is listed as one labor-day, regardless of the level of skill or efficiency. Those of youth groups and teen-age children of the members are recorded as some fixed proportion of a work-day, as stipulated by the rules of the Audit Union. Finally, and most important, the total money cost of consumption expenditures on the one hand, and the total number of work-days in the income-producing branches, on the other hand, having been determined, the "cost" of a labor-day in a particular kibbutz can be computed by dividing the former figure by the latter. Since in each income-producing branch records have been kept of its sales, production expenditures, and labor-days, these can then be converted to their money equivalent, and the profit or loss of that branch in the previous fiscal year can be computed. This has the effect of stimulating the head of that particular department and his staff to greater effort in order to show the kibbutz that "his" or "their" branch is the most profitable. Comparative studies of similar departments in other kibbutzim with similar conditions by the economic manager and his committee would inform them whether their particular branches were managed as well as those in others, and to seek corrective measures where theirs were less efficient. With the development of the national kibbutz federations, experts are being dispatched to their various collectives (especially to the younger, weaker settlements) to aid in planning and management. Since the middle 1950's, the National Productivity Institute, set up by the government to raise productivity in the economy, has been aiding the settlements in their efforts towards greater efficiency.

More recently, many leading members have expressed opposition to this type of computation of profit and loss for the income-producing divisions. A negative attitude has arisen with respect to the service branches, even toward those departments such as the machine shop for repairs, storage, and others which are essential for the proper functioning of the economy yet show no profit, or even losses. Exteme and absurd situations have occurred where the head of a branch balked at "selling" his produce to the kitchen manager in his kibbutz, because he was convinced that the "price" equivalent which the Audit Union had set for "internally-sold" products was much below the price paid by Tnuva and that this "discount" lowered the profitability of "his" branch. The division raising animal fodder might be relatively unprofitable, while that concerned with dairy and poultry which it serves showed sizeable profits. There are branches which utilize labor in the "slack" season, and, since the true marginal cost of labor is essentially lower than the average cost computed for the collective economy as a whole, they would be deemed profitable if they would be "charged" with their marginal costs, rather than with the average cost of labor in that particular kibbutz. These various criticisms have brought about suggestions in the direction of considering the collective economy as a whole as one accounting unit, yet retaining statistical data on the labor-days and expenditures incurred in each branch, without the elaborate computation of profit and loss of each. These data would guide management in seeking improved efficiency.[20]

For the kibbutz as a whole, the concept of profit or loss is equivalent to saving or dissaving in a household. In the case of a business enterprise, the prices of the productive factors are generally given to it by the market. The accounting system of the collective determines the labor costs of the income-producing branches, not by the equivalent labor costs in the national economy, but by the consumption levels and the efficiency of the service branches. Thus, profits (i.e., saving) could be increased, not necessarily by improving the efficiency of the income-producing branches, but by lowering consumption costs (and therefore the labor costs of the income-producing branches). If the number of children increases, thus raising consumption costs, the income-producing branches which had previously shown a profit might then show a loss, not because they had become less efficient, but because the cost of a labor-day in that kibbutz had increased. What is more, the increased number of children will necessitate (especially under the collective setup) increased labor-days in the consumption branches, reducing those available to the productive branches, requiring a curtailment of production or increased costs through the hiring of outside labor. All these factors must be kept in mind when analyzing the profitability (or lack of it) of the collective economy.

The early period of kibbutz history is one of almost constant losses. The decade of the 1920's was one of severe deflation in Palestine, resulting in a great increase in the burden of the debts and a concomitant decline in income. The lack of general agricultural experience, particularly in the management of a collective economy, made for severe losses and economic hardships. In the mid-1930's, however, the older kibbutzim began to show a profit in certain years. But it was the prosperity arising from the large-scale immigration of Jews fleeing Nazi Germany, and the inflation accompanying World War II, that reversed the process of the 1920's. The inflationary erosion of debt burdens, increased demand, and higher prices enabled the collectives to start some modest accumulation of capital. The first years of the State and the mass immigration saw an acceleration of inflationary pressures. Thus in 1950, the kibbutzim as a whole showed a ratio of profit (saving) to net income of 5.9 per cent, and in the older kibbutzim it averaged 9.3 per cent.[21]

In 1952, the government instituted a "New Economic Policy" which included a drastic devaluation of the Israeli pound. At the same time, it raised reserve requirements of the banks considerably, so that credit rationing became very stringent. The newer kibbutzim were especially affected as they were in the process of developing their economies at a time when the cost of investment more than doubled, and the availability of credit was severely restricted. Even the older collectives found themselves encountering growing financial difficulties on account of their usual expansionist tendencies, as well as the need for short-term capital to finance current production. The rationing of imported equipment and raw materials (constituting the bulk of investment goods) added to the problems of both investment and current production, and the control of prices of agricultural produce made budget balancing very difficult for many settlements.

Income. In 1949, gross income of the kibbutzim from agriculture was 58.8 per cent of total income; from non-agricultural enterprises within the collectives, 22.8 per cent; from national or regional trucking and bus cooperatives in which the collectives owned shares and to which the collectives sent their drivers, 8.4 per cent; and from outside work, 10 per cent (this includes not only salaries of members working for governmental and other agencies, but also the renting of agricultural equipment to other settlements, repairs done at the kibbutz workshops for other settlements, etc.). The large expansion in agriculture, induced by the increased demand accompanying the mass immigration, and the great increase in the number of new collectives during the first few years following Israeli independence, which were based wholly on agriculture, made this sector even more important in the economy of the kibbutzim. As farm surpluses began to appear in the mid-1950's, the trend towards industrialization of the kibbutz economy began to reassert itself. Thus in 1954, the ratios of gross income were the following: agriculture, 77.1 per cent; non-agricultural enterprises within the kibbutz, 15 per cent; transport, 3.9 per cent; outside work, 4.0 per cent.[22] Since that date, the trend indicated is for a smaller share of income derived from farming and a larger share from non-agricultural sources. Obviously, this does not follow a smooth, continuous course, so that in years where "natural factors" favor agriculture its importance rises, and conversely in years of drought or other adverse factors, other sources of income are more pronounced. (As the collectives increasingly rely upon irrigated agriculture, these fluctuations are minimized.) Thus the report of the Ihud Federation of 1961 indicates that the ratio between agricultural and industrial gross income was 5:2, not including income from rest homes maintained by many kibbutzim, repairs for other settlements, and other non-agricultural income. Hakibbutz Ha'artzi Federation reports a 2:1 ratio of agricultural to industrial income (again excluding rest homes and other non-agricultural income).[23] Hakibbutz Hameuhad Federation reports that about 25 per cent of their gross income in 1962 was derived from manufacturing. If one should add other non-agricultural income, it would probably be at least a third of their total income.[24] Of course, even in the first half of the decade of the 1950's, when the role of agriculture became increasingly important in the kibbutz movement as a whole, there were sharp differences between one settlement and another, and the agricultural sector in older, established kibbutzim was much less preponderant.

One cannot overemphasize the fact that these broad generalizations regarding the kibbutz economy conceal major differences between one settlement and another. The main variables determining these inter-kibbutz differences would seem to be the age of the kibbutz and its regional location. It has already been indicated that as the collectives become more established they tend to increase the emphasis upon non-agricultural enterprises, though there are still a few settlements which "ideologically" have maintained their refusal to "turn the kibbutz into a factory." Though agricultural diversification is an economic principle espoused by the leadership of the movement, one finds certain sections where kibbutzim derive as much as 40 per cent, and even more, of their gross income from agriculture from one branch. Thus some kibbutzim in the Beisan Valley where the water supply is plentiful may derive 40 per cent of their gross agricultural income from their fish ponds. Kibbutzim in the hot Jordan Valley frequently derive over 40 per cent of their gross agricultural income from the banana crop. Those few kibbutzim which were settled in the Sharon (the populous coastal area where most of Israel's citrus crop is grown) often derive 40 or 50 per cent of their income from agriculture from the citrus crop alone. Yet these examples should be considered atypical, for in most cases the collectives have four or five agricultural branches which dominate their agricultural economy and one or more industrial branches, plus the various service divisions necessary for the operation of these enterprises.

Expenditures. Expenditures of the kibbutz are subdivided into five broad categories: direct money expenditures on consumption; production costs such as seed, fertilizer, etc.; administrative costs; interest payments; and depreciation allowances. Labor-days are recorded separately. The trend since the early 1950's (primarily after the institution of the New Economic Policy) seems to be for relatively larger increases in production expenditures and interest costs and a consequent lower ratio of consumption costs to total expenditures. This trend is also evidenced by the worsening parity index of agriculture, with costs of inputs in agriculture rising much more than prices of outputs. This tends to restrain the rise of food prices and of some other consumption goods, but worsens the profitability of agriculture. Thus between 1953 and 1956 consumption outlays declined from 42.1 per cent of total money expenditures to 33.6 per cent. Conversely, production costs increased from 41.7 to 48.4 per cent. Administrative costs were relatively stable at 4.6 per cent of total money expenditures. However, interest costs continued to rise at a rapid pace, from 4.3 per cent in 1953 to 7.5 per cent in 1956.[25] All the evidence indicates that this rise in interest costs has been continuing; in the older settlements it had risen to 9.3 per cent in 1957.[26] In 1959, interest costs were 10.1 per cent of gross income of the older kibbutzim, compared with 6.3 per cent five years earlier.[27] Another study of the collectives shows that interest costs rose from 3.1 per cent of gross income in 1953 to 9 per cent in 1961.[28] Since this study embraces all the collectives and since approximately 100 of the 228 kibbutzim were "directed kibbutzim" (receiving low-interest, long-term loans from the Jewish Agency), it would indicate that interest costs in the other settlements are much higher. This is borne out by a study of 24 established collectives where the average interest costs in 1960 were 15 per cent of their gross production.[29]

Depreciation allowances as shown in the accounts of the kibbutzim are not very meaningful, since they are based on the historical costs of their assets rather than on replacement cost. The severe devaluation of the Israeli pound in 1952 and the more recent devaluation in 1962 make the evaluation of assets as carried in their accounts quite meaningless. This problem will be dealt with more fully in the analysis of profitability of the collectives.

Comparing the older, larger, well-established settlements with their younger, smaller, and weaker counterparts, it is evident that both money-expenditures and labor-days are considerably higher in the latter on a per member basis, both for adult food and clothing. This is by no means indicative of higher consumption standards — if anything, the reverse would be true. The established collectives produce a much higher percentage of their food and clothing requirements at "discount" prices, are more experienced in management, and have modern equipment and laundry facilities which enable them to economize both on money-expenditures and labor-days. On the other hand, in terms of expenditure on children per worker (not per child) the younger kibbutzim with fewer children in the early years of settlement spent much less than did the developed kibbutzim. It is this major difference which enables the younger to compete, so to speak, with the older settlements. For, although they are generally less efficient, due to inexperience, less equipment per worker, and smaller-scale operations, their smaller number of children lowers their *total* cost of upkeep which, as pointed out earlier, means lower labor costs in the income-producing branches, as well as a higher proportion of their labor force in the productive branches of the economy.

IV

THE CHANGING POSITION OF THE KIBBUTZIM IN THE NATIONAL ECONOMY

Since the Israeli collective is a very active unit in the social, economic, and political life of the country, inevitably it is strongly influenced by the dynamic economy and society of Israel. This is true of the kibbutz both as a producing unit and as a consuming unit. Thus the trend within the kibbutz economy towards an increasing emphasis upon non-agricultural pursuits reflects a similar development within the national economy. Similarly, the rapid rise in living levels in the collectives since the early 1950's is a reflection of similar trends within Israeli society.

AGRICULTURE

With the cessation of hostilities in 1948, the complete break in trade relations with the neighboring Arab countries (which had previously supplied Palestine with agricultural produce), and the mass immigration of Jews from Europe and the Arab countries, the government of Israel adopted a policy of rapid expansion of the agricultural sector. This was in keeping with the training and convictions of the kibbutz movement, which had always viewed agricultural pursuits as the "noblest" form of human endeavor. The new government came into possession of large uncultivated and abandoned areas, especially in the south. Pending the use of these lands for the founding of new settlements, they were, in most cases, temporarily leased to the collectives. The kibbutzim had both the "know-how" and the mechanized equipment. They had, for example, over 80 per cent of all the tractors in Israel in 1949. As new settlements mushroomed, the bulk of which were moshavim, the kibbutz share of Israel's cultivated area declined from 45.7 per cent in 1949 to 34.3 per cent in 1963. In absolute terms the cultivated area of the kibbutzim increased until 1952, and has, thereafter, remained rather constant (see Appendix III).

This has been a strong factor in inducing the kibbutzim to turn increasingly towards irrigation. For the period 1949–1960 the rate of growth of the irrigated area was extremely high in Israeli agriculture as a whole, though the pace has slowed down since the appearance of surpluses in the middle and later 1950's. The kibbutz share of Israel's irrigated area increased from one-fourth in 1949 to one-third in 1963. In view of the fact that the kibbutz share of Israel's agricultural labor force has been declining, their increasing share of the irrigated area is all the more noteworthy (see Appendix IV).

The fruit plantations constitute a major area of kibbutz investment. Between 1949 and 1963, the area of fruit plantations (most of which are irrigated) more than doubled in the country and more than quadrupled in the kibbutz sector. The kibbutz share of Israel's fruit plantations rose from over 9 per cent in 1949 to 18 per cent in 1963. In the initial period, however, the collectives emphasized most of the non-citrus fruits. Since the market for these fruits is largely domestic, whereas the bulk of the citrus crop is grown for export, the collectives have suffered from the large surpluses that have become commonplace since the later 1950's. They have, therefore, shifted their emphasis towards citriculture because of its profitability, as well as the fact that areas other than the coastal region (where there are few kibbutzim) were found to be suitable for this crop (see Appendix V).

The large tracts of land allocated to the collectives following Israeli independence were used mostly for unirrigated field crops. Thus 55 per cent of all of Israel's field crops were cultivated by the kibbutzim in 1949. As the moshav movement developed very rapidly, and as the kibbutzim themselves laid increasing stress on intensive agriculture, the kibbutz share of Israel's field crops declined to 40 per cent in 1963; this decline was both absolute and relative since 1959 (see Appendix VI). A similar development has taken place in the area of vegetable crops. The kibbutzim have progressively abandoned this branch due mainly to their severe manpower shortage, the opposition within the movement to the use of hired labor, the inability to mechanize many operations, and the frequent surpluses of vegetables. Thus the kibbutz share of Israel's area of vegetable production declined from 18 per cent in 1949 to 12 per cent in 1963; since 1956 this decline has been both absolute and relative (see Appendix VII).

Investment in mechanization in the collective sector far ex-

ceeded the kibbutzim's disproportionate share of the total cultivated area of Israel. In 1959 they had 41 per cent of all the
tractors in Israel, while their share of the cultivated area was 34
per cent. Tractors, especially the increasingly popular wheeled
tractors, are used for hauling as well as for field work. The kibbutz share of Israel's grain combines was 64 per cent in 1959, and
83 per cent of the more expensive self-propelled model. This was
far more than their share of Israel's field crops which was 43
per cent in that year. Their share of the total number of balers
has been rather constant since the mid-1950's (53% in 1959).
Criticism was levelled at the collective sector for their over-em-
phasis on mechanization. It would seem, a priori, that with a
rational utilization of equipment — given the advantage the kibbutz has in its possession of large contiguous plots of land (as
compared with the small moshav farmer) — the collective would
require fewer tractors per cultivated dunam than the other sectors.
It should be noted, however, that the collectives were constantly
reducing their number of work animals, while in other sectors
they were increasing. Furthermore, the collectives rent their agricultural equipment, together with their operators, to other farms.

Data for 1963 indicate that the greater rate of mechanization in
the non-kibbutz agricultural sectors in recent years has further
reduced the relative share of the kibbutz sector. Thus the collectives owned 33 per cent of Israel's tractors as compared with
their possession of 34 per cent of Israel's cultivated area; their
share of grain combines was 43 per cent and of balers 33 per cent.
In the case of tractors, there was a small increase in 1963 (as compared with 1959) and an absolute decrease in the number of
combines and balers. It seems that the financial stringency in which
many kibbutzim found themselves in the 1950's (discussed in
Chapter VI) has brought about a reassessment of investment
planning and put a brake on the rate of mechanization. This has
probably resulted in the more efficient use of equipment.

The dairy and poultry branches have assumed an increasingly
important role in Israeli agriculture. The reasons for this development are primarily the relatively high income elasticity of their
products, their liquidity, and their higher profitability. The following data relate to the Jewish agricultural sector, but the conclusions would be substantially the same, taking into account the
non-Jewish sector. The Jewish sector produced 96 per cent of
the total value of cow's milk in 1949 and 98.1 per cent in 1963.

Similarly, the Jewish sector provided 98.8 per cent of Israel's egg production in 1949 and 99.3 per cent in 1963.

In 1963 the number of dairy cattle in Israel was triple their number in 1949, while in the kibbutzim the herd was two and one-third times as large. The result was that the kibbutz share declined from 39 per cent in 1949 to 28 per cent in 1963, but the latter figure understates the role of the kibbutz since the yields and efficiency are generally superior in the collectives (see Appendix VIII). In the poultry branch, the kibbutz share of Israel's laying hens was 11.6 per cent in 1949 and 14.4 per cent in 1963. The mere summation of the period does not reveal the considerable shifts within that period. Until 1954 there was a strict rationing of feed imposed by the government to conserve foreign exchange. Price controls on eggs and meat were in force, but the kibbutzim with their large areas of field crops were able to raise most of their own feed, and were therefore much less affected by the import restrictions. The result was a sharp expansion of the poultry branch in the collectives and a contraction in the private sector. Beginning with 1954, there was a gradual relaxation of these controls until their abolition in 1956. The rapidly expanding moshav movement found this branch most attractive and invested heavily in poultry. As surpluses appeared in the later 1950's in dairy and poultry, the farmers were vociferous in their demand for government subsidies. Since that time, the government has used the subsidy program as a weapon for restricting the growth of dairy and poultry. It has severely restricted the poultry branch and has, until recently, allowed a very limited expansion of dairy production (see Appendix IX).

Another reason for the shift in the poultry branch toward the private sector is the much higher cost of investment in the modern "American" type of chicken coop prevalent in the collective settlements. In 1957 it was estimated that the cost of such "housing" investment per laying hen was IL 36 in the kibbutzim as compared with IL 11 for the simpler type of coops used in the moshavim. The family farm can utilize women's and children's labor in this branch. While it is true that production per workday in the collective is three times that in the moshav, the use of family labor in the private sector more than offsets this advantage. Furthermore, investment in the poultry branch is of a relatively liquid nature, in terms of the time lag from the date of investment to the receipt of income, making it especially attractive to the family farm. The result has been a surplus of poultry products, a drain on the foreign exchange reserves of the Treasury, as well as subsidization of production. In terms of *private* profitability, it has made the established family farms specializing in this branch very successful economic units.[1]

The high rate of investment of the collective sector in irrigation, mechanical equipment, and other capital goods, as well as invest-ment in "human capital" in terms of acquisition of skills and ex-perience, has enabled the kibbutzim to maintain their important position in terms of gross agricultural production in Israel. In 1949 they produced 27.6 per cent of Israel's gross agricultural production and in 1960, 31.3 per cent. Over the twelve-year period, 1949–1960, the average annual rate of growth of agricul-tural production in the collective sector was 16.3 per cent; in the rest of Israeli agriculture, 13.6 per cent. Taking the last six years of this period, 1955–1960, when the agricultural labor force was more or less constant in the kibbutzim and increased approximate-ly 23 per cent in the private sector, the average annual rate of growth of gross production was 14 per cent in the kibbutzim and 12.4 per cent in non-collective agriculture (see Appendix X). Table 6 summarizes the position of the collective sector within the agricultural sector in Israel as a whole in 1960.

Recent estimates of agricultural production in the collectives between 1960 and 1964 indicate an annual rate of growth of 9.6 per cent in the kibbutz sector as compared with 7.8 per cent in the rest of Israeli agriculture, thus raising their share to almost one-third of the total. It would seem that this was due to the fruition of large-scale investment in collective agriculture in previous years, as well as greater efficiency and productivity.

As a result of the increasing surpluses of many agricultural products, primarily in the poultry, dairy, and vegetable branches, farmers have been subjected to increasing production controls. An expansion of exports could reduce these surpluses; but, in the case of most agricultural exports, other than citrus, local costs of production exceed international prices at the prevailing ex-change rate. Another alternative is to decrease imports of goods which can be locally produced. This has been done, but at a cost of production in excess of the imported products. The introduc-tion of industrial crops is looked upon as an "infant industry," the theory being that with the accumulation of experience Israeli agriculture will be able to lower costs of production to the international level. In the case of orchards, the large surpluses have brought about a governmental regulation forbidding the planting of fruit trees without a permit. There is, on the other hand, considerable pressure exerted by the "farm lobby" to forbid all imports of agricultural products which can be produced locally regardless of price. The Jewish Agency's Settlement Department is continually pressing in favor of increased production quotas for those settlements under its aegis, especially the newer settlements; this tends to increase productive capacity. It is important, therefore, to distinguish between "social" profitability and "private" profitability, though frequently the two concepts are concurrent. In this regard, a study made by the Audit Union for Cooperative Agriculture found that in the livestock branches in the collectives in 1957 purchased feedstuffs (generally imported) were 35 per cent of the total used, whereas in the other sectors of Jewish agriculture it was 54 per cent.[2] Of interest also is the fact that non-irrigated field crops, which are strongest in the kibbutzim, are beneficial to the national economy in terms of international prices.[3]

The Horowitz Committee, a governmental commission appointed to study the problems of Israeli agriculture, found that in 1956 the prices of certain goods were below the international import prices and others, above these prices. The price of citrus was 46 per cent of the international price; tobacco (produced mainly in the Arab sector), 59 per cent; peanuts, 83 per cent; poultry meat, 86 per cent; eggs, equal in price; barley, 4 per cent higher; wheat, 11 per cent higher; corn, 8 per cent higher; cotton, 17 per cent higher; sugar beets, 46 per cent higher; milk, 43 per cent higher; and other products still higher.[4] Of course, the import content of the locally produced goods, which is particularly high in the livestock branches, must be considered. The prices were based on an exchange rate of IL 2.650 to the dollar. In view of the increasing efficiency of Israeli agriculture, the new exchange rate of three Israeli pounds to the dollar (1962), the incipient stage of "industrial" crops, such as cotton, sugar beets, and peanuts in 1956, and the increasing experience of Israel's farmers, it is likely that many more agricultural goods will become competitive with the international market prices. A glance at the data in Table 6 indicates the importance to the economy of Israel of the branches in which the kibbutzim specialize — primarily, field crops.

NON-AGRICULTURAL ENTERPRISES

In contrast with the development of collective agriculture, which was originally stimulated by the pioneering Zionist ideology of the youth movements, the development of kibbutz industry was aided by a combination of economic factors. Initially, the establishment of such branches as machine shops, carpentry shops, and others was designed to serve the needs of the economy of the collective. The distances from urban centers made these essential for the increasingly mechanized agricultural economy. Even those settlements located near urban centers found it economical to provide their own services rather than to purchase them elsewhere. Some of the more venturesome branch managers found that they could accept outside work from other settlements in the neighborhood and thus increase their incomes and profitability. The severe limitations of land and water prior to 1948 were a strong inducement to seek non-agricultural enterprises which would provide income and employment for their growing membership. This transition came about without the encouragement or aid of the Jewish settlement authorities, whose policies remained the traditional Zionist ones. With the colonization of the Negev, they began to recognize the need to introduce industry in these settlements.

Of the three large kibbutz federations, Hakibbutz Hameuhad and Hakibbutz Ha'artzi were early advocates of this change and made concerted efforts to develop industrial enterprises in their affiliated collectives even without the aid of the settlement authorities of the Jewish Agency. Often these enterprises became large-scale establishments and were set up as separate corporate entities. In many cases, private capitalists were sold shares in these corporations, though the collectives would retain majority control. In other cases, they were jointly owned corporations of a number of neighboring settlements. The third large kibbutz federation, the Ihud, began the development of non-agricultural enterprises at a later stage.

Before 1948 the collective settlements were dependent upon outside employment for a considerable part of their income, since the land shortage inhibited agricultural development. The cyclical and seasonal fluctuations of the general labor market made their economic position precarious. Even the more established kibbutzim of that era found that their agricultural economies were subject to seasonal labor changes. The expansion of industrial enterprises by these collectives was looked upon as a mere extension of the "tenet" of a diversified economy, smoothing the pattern of labor requirements, as well as of fluctuations in income receipts.[5]

In addition to the kibbutzim which before 1948 had been allocated a certain amount of land and a budget necessary for permanent settlement, there were many "Kibbutzei Avodah." These were groups which had organized in or near the main urban centers and lived "collectively," mainly working as employees of the private enterprise economy and pooling their incomes. These groups frequently had to wait a number of years before being permanently settled in outlying parts of the country. Meanwhile, some of them developed small-scale enterprises to employ their members. The incentive was not only the possibility of greater profit than that offered by the alternative wage income, but also the frequency of periods of general unemployment that prevailed in Palestine. When these groups did finally settle, they would often develop these small-scale enterprises on a larger and more permanent basis. Other groups in this category trained themselves as building contractors or subcontractors, which skills were later used in their permanent settlement site.

World War II provided a strong stimulus to the development of industry in the country as a whole as well as in the kibbutzim. The difficulty of importing from abroad set up a most effective protective barrier for the growth of local industry. Orders from the Allied armies in the Middle East substantially aided this process, for the kibbutzim, which were among the important suppliers of agricultural produce, found that they could increase their profits by canning their produce for sale. During this period, the kibbutz movement began to look upon their industrial enterprises, not merely as adjuncts to their agricultural economies, supplementing total income and providing employment in the "off" season in agriculture, but as enterprises worthy of development in their own right. Thus in 1943, the very oldest kibbutzim (those established before 1927) had 11 per cent of their labor force employed in industry and derived 21.3 per cent of their gross income from that source. The kibbutzim established between the years 1928 and 1932 had 24.5 per cent of their labor force employed in industrial enterprises and derived 58.1 per cent of their gross income from that source in 1943. Those settlements founded between 1936 and 1938 had 10.3 per cent of their labor force employed in industry. By 1947 these industries had further developed, but the cessation of the war diminished their rate of growth and enabled a relatively greater rate of growth of their agricultural branches. It should be noted that even during these years of rapid industrial growth the development of these branches was not at the "expense" of the agricultural sector, but was because of a diminution in the number of members in outside employment.

A survey of industrial enterprises in the kibbutzim in 1947 showed 126 establishments employing 1,153 workers. In addition, some of the settlements in cooler parts of the country had developed so-called rest homes, or, more accurately, vacation centers, for the population at large, which proved to be quite lucrative. There were eight such establishments in 1947, employing about 250 people. The kibbutzim had also developed trucking cooperatives which usually took the form of partnerships of a number of settlements in a particular region and served the general population of the area as well as the collectives. In terms of the employed labor force, the food industries constituted 26.5 per cent of the total (other than rest homes and trucking cooperatives). These included canning, the manufacture of glucose, jams, and biscuits, large regional bakeries, flour mills, the manufacture of animal feed and other items. Another 24 per cent of the kibbutz industrial labor force was employed in metal works. These included the manufacture of agricultural machinery (other than tractors, combines and "heavy" equipment), the manufacture of irrigation equipment, water meters, electrical equipment, kitchen equipment, etc., and major repair shops for trucks and agricultural machinery. Another 19.4 per cent was in the woodwork branches producing furniture, doors, windows. The other 30 per cent included printing, leather works, building materials, chemicals and other items.[6]

With the establishment of the State of Israel in 1948, the trend towards industrialization was temporarily restrained, because the authorities were strongly encouraging agriculture. The $35 million loan given by the Export-Import Bank of the U.S. government to the Israeli government was solely for the development of Israeli agriculture. Agricultural machinery and irrigation equipment literally flowed into the country. Initially, this increase in the allocation of resources to agriculture did not impinge upon the industrial sector but accelerated the decline in the number of collective members employed outside the kibbutzim. By 1951, however, the relative position of industry in the collective sector began to decline (though in the absolute sense it continued to grow). Beginning with 1955, the appearance of agricultural surpluses in Israel brought about a reassertion of the previous trend towards increased relative (and absolute) growth of non-agricultural kibbutz enterprises.

In addition to the previously mentioned causes for the increasing shift towards industrialization of the kibbutz economy — especially declining profitability of agriculture since the mid-1950's — there was another factor that began to affect the collective movement, namely, the increasing percentage of older members. In 1948, the fifteen to twenty-nine-year-old age group in the kibbutzim was 40.4 per cent of the total population of the collectives, compared with 24.1 per cent in Israel as a whole.[7] Since that time there has been a general aging of the population in the collectives. In the early pre-State period of kibbutz history, the continual large influx of young people from the pioneering movements abroad kept the average age level of the labor force considerably below that prevalent in the country as a whole. Since then, also, the number of new recruits has dwindled. With the exodus of many members, primarily those in their twenties or thirties, and with some of the younger children of the kibbutz members leaving the movement when they complete their service in the armed forces, the kibbutzim are increasingly faced with a problem of an aging population. Generally speaking, the older members are more adapted to industrial work, especially in light industry, than to the more arduous labor of farming. This is one of the problems which has been occupying the planners of the kibbutz movement of late.[8] From 1,153 employees in industry in 1947, there was an increase to 3,303 in 1952, and by 1954 there were more than 4,000 workers in these enterprises. These figures do not include employees in the rest homes and the transport cooperatives.[9]

Organization. In terms of organization, one might subdivide kibbutz industry into two broad categories. The smaller enterprises are generally considered an integral part of the collective economy. They have no separate existence in the legal or economic sense. The budget is part of the general budget and is managed by a branch manager as is any other branch of the economy, under the supervision of the general Secretariat. The larger enterprises are independent units, often incorporated. In many cases, these are owned by a number of neighboring kibbutzim, or by the kibbutz and private capital, or jointly with the Jewish Agency or the Histadrut, or some combination of these. In these cases, the kibbutz receives the wages of its members employed in the industry in addition to its share of the profits. The non-kibbutz members employed in these enterprises are paid in accordance with the union scale as determined nationally by the Histadrut. This includes fringe benefits. Management of these enterprises is usually in the hands of a committee of three or four members, each with his particular functions and duties. Usually one of these members becomes the over-all *de facto* manager. With regards to market behavior there is little to distinguish kibbutz and private industry. Kibbutz industry takes part in cartels and syndicates which control prices and share markets, certainly to the extent that these are legal in Israel.[10]

Subdividing industry and crafts into three categories in terms of the employed labor force, the data for 1958 show that 52 per cent of the industrial labor force of the kibbutzim was in the smallest type of establishment, most frequently repair shops, compared with 28 per cent in Israel as a whole. In the industrial establishments employing less than 50 workers, 17 per cent of the kibbutz labor force was in this type of establishment compared with 38 per cent in this category in Israel as a whole. In the large industrial establishments (in Israeli terms) employing 50 or more workers, 31 per cent of the collective industrial labor force was in this category, compared with 34 per cent for Israel as a whole. In terms of fixed assets and equipment per worker, it would seem that collective enterprise was on a level approximating that of the industrial establishments of Israel as a whole.[11]

Gross Production. Gross production in the kibbutz industries has been increasing beyond the considerable rate of growth prevalent in Israeli industry. For example, in 1951 gross industrial production of the kibbutzim was 3.1 per cent of the Israeli total; in 1955, it was 4.2 per cent; in 1959, it had reached 5.8 per cent of gross industrial production in Israel. These figures include the large number of repair shops in the kibbutzim which cannot, strictly speaking, be classified as industrial establishments. Excluding this category, the position of kibbutz industrial production in 1959 would be 4.3 per cent instead of the above-mentioned 5.8 per cent of the Israeli total.

A survey of all kibbutz industrial establishments employing five or more workers in 1960 (excluding the small repair shops in the kibbutzim) revealed that the number employed in these establishments had increased almost 10 per cent since the previous year, though the number of such enterprises had increased by one (from 118 in 1959 to 119 in 1960). Table 7 gives the results of the 1960 survey.

An estimate made for 1962 stated that the number of industrial establishments in the kibbutzim had increased to 130 and the number employed to approximately 6,000, and gross production had reached IL 150 million. (The latter figure must be corrected for inflationary price increases to be comparable with the 1960 data in Table 7.[12]) This rapid pace of industrialization is further corroborated by the Bank of Israel report for 1961.[13]

TABLE 7. SURVEY OF MANUFACTURING IN THE KIBBUTZIM IN 1960

PRODUCT	NO. OF ESTABLISH- MENTS	NO. OF WORKERS	GROSS PRO- DUCTION IN IL 1,000	WAGES AND SALARIES IN IL 1,000
Food and tobacco	23	1,124	23,187	3,890
Textiles	6	106	1,487	380
Wood products	20	1,766	29,765	7,048
Printing	7	194	1,880	978
Leather	4	146	1,811	575
Rubber and plastics	3	140	4,048	619
Chemicals and oil	2	167	5,673	901
Non-ferrous metals	5	299	4,392	1,258
Metal works	4	115	2,259	462
Metal products	14	573	10,172	2,331
Machinery	18	364	4,670	1,256
Transportation equipment	4	112	1,187	398
Mines and sand	3	25	589	99
Miscellaneous	6	200	3,729	987
Total	119	5,331	94,394	21,182

Source: Cooperative Almanac of Israel (Tel Aviv, 1962), p. 77.

Note: Only plants with five or more workers were included in this survey.

In a memorandum issued by the Kibbutz Industries Association in March 1965, a total of 151 non-agricultural enterprises are mentioned including 20 vacation resorts. Gross production in 1963 is estimated as IL 200 million or 5 per cent of Israel's industrial production. In addition there were 35 inter-kibbutz regional plants for the processing of agricultural products, with a capital investment of IL 66 million, and gross production of IL 63 million. Most kibbutz industries employ 35 to 40 workers, though there are nine which employ between 100 and 550 workers.

Sample surveys of industrial establishments conducted by the Central Bureau of Statistics show that in 1956 kibbutz enterprises constituted 1.5 per cent of the total and employed 2.4 per cent of Israel's industrial labor force. In 1964, establishments in collective settlements constituted 1.2 per cent of the total, but the percentage of the industrial labor force employed by the kibbutzim had increased to 3.4 per cent. This would seem to indicate that the size of the collective enterprises (measured by the number employed) increased much faster than in Israel as a whole. The percentage of employed persons in enterprises with 50 or more workers had risen from 41 per cent in 1956 to 53 per cent in 1964 (in Israel).

Hired Labor. However, while economic considerations, primarily the declining parity index and the worsening profitability of agriculture, impelled the collective settlements to place increasing emphasis upon non-agricultural enterprises, this has created, or at least intensified, non-economic problems for the settlements, principally the problem of hired labor. The estimate for 1963 was that about two-thirds of the 6,000 workers employed in kibbutz industry were hired laborers. Unlike agriculture, which enjoys a considerable degree of governmental protection (as in most Western developed countries), the kibbutz feels the full brunt of competition of the private industrial sector of Israel, as well as the increasing liberalization of imported industrial goods. Furthermore, industry is constantly increasing its scale of operations so as to lower costs and compete with foreign producers. In agriculture, the kibbutz is the large-scale producer in Israel and enjoys considerable advantages in terms of economies of scale and a high degree of specialization and technology, but in industry it enjoys no such advantages. The strong opposition of the kibbutz movement to hired labor provides a most serious obstacle to further expansion in the scale of its industrial operations. Although kibbutz publications have reported opinions which justify hired labor (other than for "menial" tasks), these are not numerous,[14] and the official stand is to eliminate it as soon as possible. Yet, the movement realizes that while hired labor might possibly be eliminated in their agricultural branches, the necessity to increase the scale of operations in their existing industries (even should they refrain from establishing new ones) make it well-nigh impossible to hope for such a development in their industrial sector. The problems which hired labor creates within the collective are manifold. The members who had at all times considered themselves as part and parcel of the "working class" are now managers and "exploiters." One observer has noted that the exodus of members from kibbutzim is greatest in those settlements where hired labor is most prevalent.[15] Others have noted that the second generation growing up in the collectives fails to see the difference between kibbutz life and other forms of social and economic organization.[16] What is probably worse is the lack of any job security which the hired laborers have, since they are aware of the fact that the collectives only employ them until they can replace them with one of their own members. This basic antagonism recently led to a strike on the part of the hired workers against their kibbutz employers.[17]

One suggested solution to this dilemma has been the conversion of these industries into cooperatives, jointly owned by the kibbutz and the permanent staff of hired workers. One kibbutz has, in fact, begun to adopt this method of solving its problems with hired labor. It has a large establishment for the manufacture of doors, in which IL 1.1 million has been invested by the kibbutz, with a regular staff of 10 kibbutz members and 25 hired workers. The kibbutz retains 70 per cent of the shares of the cooperative, and the 25 hired workers are offered shares in the cooperative at IL 5,000 per share. The kibbutz will arrange to seek the necessary loans to help these workers pay for their shares.[18]

This solution is opposed, however, by the leadership of the three major kibbutz federations, and no alternative has been found. One report mentions that a certain kibbutz, which receives almost double the wage-rate from its members employed in its industrial enterprise as compared with that which it pays its hired workers (though it pays the Histadrut wage scale), forwards the difference to a special fund of its kibbutz federation.[19] Some kibbutz leaders suggest the establishment of corporations jointly owned by the kibbutz (or a few kibbutzim) together with the Histadrut and the Jewish Agency and possibly the government, and that the kibbutz should employ its own members in these enterprises only in proportion to its ownership of the firm, so that the hired laborers would, in effect, be the employees of the public corporations rather than of the kibbutz. This would have the merit of not only removing the stigma of "exploitation," but also of enabling the enterprises to expand further with the capital invested in them by the corporations. This solution is opposed by the largest kibbutz federation. Hakibbutz Ha'artzi, which feels that either the workers opt to join the kibbutz or that the kibbutz movement must find other means of solving the problem.[20] At the same time, the managers of these enterprises, who must daily deal with economic problems, press for the continual expansion of "their" firms, regardless of other implications of such a policy.[21] In February 1963, the kibbutz movement as a whole set up an organization intended: (1) to initiate new industrial projects; (2) to set up a technical division with the aid of professional engineers and other technicians to advise its industries on technological and economic problems; (3) to have common representation in dealing with the government, the Histadrut, the Jewish Agency, and other institutions; and (4) to set up subgroupings of similar plants in the various kibbutzim for the purposes of consultation on common problems.[22] It would seem that this should give additional impetus towards industrialization.

Rural industrialization has more recently been adopted by the government and the Jewish Agency as the desirable solution for the mis-allocation of resources which has resulted in large agricultural surpluses. The Bank of Israel report for 1961 states that kibbutz industrialization has left its mark on the activities of the Settlement Department of the Jewish Agency and the moshav movement, which in cooperation with the government has begun to create the organizational tools for developing industrial enterprises in the moshavim.[23]

To assess possible future developments, however, requires certain caution. Although industry is the main source of income in a number of kibbutzim, this will probably not be the case in most of them within the near future. Aside from the non-economic implications, it is important to remember that the kibbutzim possess very sizeable assets in their agricultural economy, in addition to the considerable investment in terms of training and experience of the membership in agricultural pursuits. If any solutions are found to "legalize" hired labor and also to increase sources of investment capital, an acceleration of the trend towards industrialization of the kibbutz economy will undoubtedly result.

The numerous regional enterprises which are jointly owned by many settlements are not encumbered by these ideological problems (even though the ownership is often completely or mostly in the hand of the collectives) and have therefore expanded rapidly in recent years. In 1960 and 1961, twenty projects were established.[24] One of these regional cooperative projects (encompassing 38 kibbutzim in the Valley of Hefer), recently set up in an area of 150 dunams, includes many branches: large silos; alfalfa drying for feed; production of prepared animal fodder; and refrigeration plants for apples, bananas, and other fruits. It plans to expand further into metal works, storage tanks for fuel, poultry slaughtering, and other branches.[25] Furthermore, organizations of the kibbutz federations (as distinct from those directly owned by the collective settlements) employ many, if not mostly, hired laborers. Hakibbutz Hameuhad Federation owns and operates four freighters, employing many hired laborers. A new organization of one of the kibbutz federations called "Motzrei Techen," which is the marketing organization recently set up to market the industrial products of the member kibbutzim of Hakibbutz Ha'artzi, employed 30 workers in 1962, two of whom were kibbutz members.[26] These developments are a result of economic criteria dictating further industrial expansion on the one hand, and of an attempt to avoid, limit, or ameliorate the ideological and social implications of these developments on the other hand.

CONSUMPTION LEVELS

In the early years of the kibbutz movement the standard of living was definitely below that of the urban worker with equivalent skills. Until the late 1930's the consumption levels were about equal to those of the unskilled urban worker, whereas many of the kibbutz members were by that time skilled in agriculture, mechanics, or management. A study comparing the moshavim in 1934–35 with the kibbutzim indicated that the expenditure per adult (excluding housing) was approximately 15 per cent lower in the collectives. Housing conditions in the kibbutzim were extremely poor. On the other hand, expenditures per child were approximately 50 per cent higher in the kibbutzim, reflecting partly the much lower birthrate of the kibbutzim, partly the institutional setup of the collective which results in higher expenditures per child, and the strong traditional emphasis in the collectives upon high levels of child care and education.[27]

Food. After the outbreak of World War II in 1939, price

controls were imposed and implemented more effectively on agricultural produce than they were on goods which the collectives bought in the general market. The result was a regression from the consumption levels of 1939. Taking food expenditures alone, one finds that (after adjustment for price changes) they had declined in two years to 72 per cent of their 1939 level. Thereafter, they began to rise again but never reached their 1939 level until a decade later in 1949. The mass immigration and the consequent austerity program imposed by the Israeli government brought a repetition of the experience of the 1940's in the early 1950's. In 1950 the real level of food expenditures had declined to 88 per cent of the 1939 level, and was further reduced to 82 per cent in the following year.[28] Of course, expenditures on food for adult members do not reflect total consumption standards. However, since the kibbutzim have traditionally held the quality of child care at a high level and most other expenditures on consumption would be reduced sooner than food expenditures, these estimates provide a barometer of changes in living standards. A further indication of the very low living standards is the percentage devoted to food items out of total expenditures. It was estimated that 50 to 65 per cent was spent on food in the 1920's and 50 to 55 per cent in the later 1930's.[29] Usually the higher the percentage of food in the budget, the lower the standard of living. Furthermore, a high percentage of caloric intake in the form of flour products is also indicative of worsening nutritional standards. Daily caloric intake declined from 3,370 in 1939 to 3,158 in 1949 and to 2,741 in 1951 when the austerity program in the country had taken effect. At the same time, the percentage of bread and other flour products in the diet declined from 40 per cent in 1939 to 26 per cent in 1949 but had risen to 29 per cent in 1951. The reverse was true for the consumption of protein and fruits and vegetables.

Housing. The kibbutz member endured very low housing standards until the late 1940's or even the early 1950's. A study made in 1937 showed that in the *older* settlements about half the membership was living in brick or cement houses averaging 2.2 adults to a small room, usually about 12 square meters (about 128 square feet); 46.2 per cent of the membership lived in prefabricated wooden houses with an average of 2.1 adults to a room (of 12 square meters); 3.6 per cent of the members (usually the newer ones) were in tents, with an average of 3.6 adults in each.[30]

In the younger settlements, the situation was far worse. In all the collectives, sanitary facilities were primitive and were centrally located for the settlement as a whole. Again, it should be emphasized that this applied only to the adult population. The children and, to a lesser extent, the elderly parents of the members enjoyed a far higher standard of nutrition, housing, and other consumption expenditures.

This serious state of affairs induced considerable investment in housing in the 1940's, especially after the end of World War II; but the increasing political tensions which were heightened as the war ended, the conflict with the Arabs, and the mass immigration had a further depressing effect on the housing situation.

The period since the early 1950's has seen a radical improvement in living standards. In the kibbutzim, and in Israel as a whole they have risen to a level estimated to approximate western European standards. In fact the collectives, which had never attained Israeli living standards, now seem to be approaching those prevailing in Israel generally. A study of expenditures on consumption between 1953 and 1957 indicates an increase in real terms of about 20 per cent, approximately the same as that of all Israel. For a family of two children, the kibbutz spent in 1958 approximately IL 250 monthly. Adjustments made for the "discount" prices which the kibbutz kitchen "pays" for internally-supplied produce, the discount which the kibbutzim receive at Hamashbir as wholesale buyers, the money-equivalent of labor services purchased by the private household, the interest costs on investment in housing in the collectives, the income tax paid by the kibbutz, and other minor items of expenditure, show consumption expenditures that equal the approximate money-equivalent of the *skilled* urban worker (taking into account taxes and social insurance which would be offset by the social security which the collective affords its members).[31] Certainly the composition of the "market basket" of goods and services offered by the collective arrangement differs considerably from that of the urban wage-earner or of the moshav cooperative farmer. In spite of recent minor modifications, the freedom of choice of each member is very limited. However, so long as he adheres to the collective mode of living, it must be assumed that he derives as much, or more, utility from this distribution of goods and services as the private family derives from its institutional arrangement. He apparently derives a high measure of satisfaction from the type of child care and education which the kibbutz provides. He values the advanced level of economic security which the collective offers him and his family and is therefore willing to forego the greater freedom of choice of the private household.

A governmental survey of annual family expenditures of urban workers made in 1956 and 1957 (with an average of 1.9 children per family) found that they averaged IL 3,122. Taking families of European or American birth with an average of 1.4 children per family, the survey showed an average annual family expenditure of IL 3,583. These sums have been adjusted for the rise in the cost of living up to September 1958, since the comparative kibbutz expenditures used are for the latter date. The budget set in September 1958 was IL 2,615 for a family of the same size. To this one must add various goods and services which the urban family purchases and which the collective provides for its members. If the price discount of internally-supplied foods and the discount which the kibbutz enjoys as a purchaser in bulk are taken into consideration, it becomes evident that the kibbutz budget per family provides for the equivalent of IL 3,263 compared with the expenditure of the established skilled urban family of IL 3,583 for a family of similar size. This excludes housing expenditures in both sectors, which, even after the very considerable improvement in kibbutz housing, would weigh the balance even more heavily in favor of the well-established urban family. There are, however, other categories of expenditure of the urban family unnecessary in the collective, such as transportation costs to and from work, life insurance, and other insurance costs. The collective pooling of risk in the kibbutz setup — which is the basic principle of any insurance — makes such insurance expenditures superfluous. Deducting IL 215 for these urban family costs (including occasional domestic help), the expenditure of the well-established urban family would be IL 3,168, as compared with the provision of IL 3,263 of goods and services by the kibbutz — not in terms of actual cost, but in terms of the equivalent cost of the urban family (again, to the exclusion of housing costs). However, these computations ignore the fact that urban living standards rose during the year and a half following the urban family survey and the fiscal year budget of the kibbutz beginning October 1, 1958. On the other hand, experience has shown that in practice the kibbutzim generally exceed the budgetary norms for consumption expenditures by 5 to 7 per cent.[32]

An analysis of the composition of expenditures of the kibbutz and the urban family indicates that the latter spent about 25 per cent more on food, even after making allowances for kibbutz price discounts. The urban family spent 14 per cent more on health, 50 per cent more on tobacco, and 18 per cent more on household furniture. In contrast, the kibbutz spent 54 per cent more on dues and other political activities (in addition to labordays, not reimbursed), and spent considerably more on education and on support of aged parents (some of whom live in the kibbutz, others live elsewhere but receive an allowance from it). In the area of clothing, cultural, and entertainment expenditures the differences were too slight to be meaningful.[33]

The large investment in housing in the collectives which took place in the 1950's has brought a quantitative as well as a qualitative change in housing standards. Moreover, an estimate published in 1959 showed that there were 1,100 vacant rooms in the kibbutzim.[34] This is due to the fact that the population of the kibbutzim had ceased to grow and had been declining between 1957 and 1961. What is less obvious is the very great change which has taken place in the quality of housing. The houses built during the 1950's have much larger rooms, usually an additional room for each kibbutz couple, as well as a veranda. Each "apartment" is provided with its own modern sanitation facilities. Many newer improvements have been introduced into the children's houses, and public buildings, including the dining hall, kitchen, community centers, synagogues, etc., are spacious and modern. Investment in sidewalks, trees, grass, and other landscaping features has given the older kibbutzim the appearance of well-to-do country or suburban communities, with features distinctive of the kibbutz communal setup. Members are provided with new furniture, radios, and other appurtenances of modern living. More recently, the kibbutzim in the hot Jordan Valley have decided to provide every family with Israeli-made "desert coolers." [35] In certain kibbutzim, kitchenettes have been installed in the private quarters of each couple, while others have gone even further and allow members to take the evening meal from the communal kitchen to their own quarters.[36] (Many kibbutzim would still consider this to be a violation of their ideological convictions.)

In spite of the rapid improvement in housing standards, however, there is still a considerable lag in this area. The younger kibbutzim and the newer members of the older settlements generally have the old wooden-frame dwellings which were vacated by the older members in favor of the newer houses. The Director of Housing of the government noted that these young members compare this with the housing available to them in the "development areas" (towns which the government is constructing in undeveloped parts of the country). He pointed out that Kiryat Gath (one of the new towns) consists mostly of ex-kibbutz members, and that relatively poor housing was one of the main causes of members leaving their kibbutzim.[37] A Department of Labor housing survey made at the end of 1958 showed that somewhat over one-half of the existing family units in the collectives were without private sanitary facilities, a relic of the old type of housing built before the 1950's.[38]

Budgets. The budget for the kibbutz family averaging 1.4 children for the fiscal year beginning October 1, 1962, was between IL 4,200 and IL 4,300. The survey of family expenditures conducted by the Central Bureau of Statistics of the government for the fiscal year beginning with October 1959, and ending September 1960 showed average expenditures per urban family (wage and salary earners) of IL 5,143 (excluding housing and property taxes) for a family of 3.8 people. The highest expenditures were in families which had immigrated from Europe and America, with an average family of 3.4 people, and expenditures of IL 6,151 annually. Adjusting for the nominal increases in personal consumption in 1961 and 1962, and correcting for the discounts and other expenditures (in accordance with Rand's estimates, previously quoted), it would seem that the consumption levels in the kibbutzim have recently not kept pace with the rapidly rising living levels in the urban sector. Rand had estimated that consumption standards in the kibbutzim in 1958 were approximately on a par with those of the higher-paid urban families which had immigrated from Europe and America (other than in housing). It would seem that the above budget for the kibbutz family for the fiscal year beginning October 1962 would indicate consumption standards which were approximately 5 per cent to 10 per cent below those of the average Jewish urban family and probably more than 25 per cent below those of the established European and American immigrants. This does not indicate a decline in kibbutz living standards. It is simply that the financial difficulties of the kibbutzim (discussed in Chapter VI) have prevented a rise in living levels commensurate with those in the prosperous urban centers. It is instructive in this regard to note that the kibbutz budget for consumption expenditure for the fiscal year beginning October 1962 are 8 per cent to 10 per cent higher than those of the previous year. This is approximately in keeping with the rise in the consumer price index in 1962. It does not allow for a real rise in the standard of living. However, in Israel as a whole, per capita consumption levels have been rising (1955 to 1964) between 5 per cent and 6 per cent annually (in real terms).

V

EFFICIENCY AND PRODUCTIVITY
OF THE KIBBUTZ ECONOMY

Analytically, the problems of productivity and profitability are distinct. Most farmers believe that the way to correct low farm income is to make adjustments in production, marketing, and credit.[1] In the case of the kibbutzim it seems that there is a definite divergence between productivity and profitability. Their productivity has generally been higher than that of the other sectors of Israeli agriculture, while the reverse is true of their profitability. This chapter concerns itself with an analysis of their productivity; the next, with profitability.

In terms of efficiency and yields the collective settlements have frequently served as pace-setters for Israeli agriculture. Of the seven prizes for productivity given to the agricultural sector by the Histadrut in 1963, six were to kibbutzim and one to an agricultural instructor in a moshav. Kibbutz Gadot developed (1) a mechanical device which doubled irrigation per man-hour in the cotton crops, and (2) a flamethrower for destroying weeds. Kibbutz Hulda took over a primitive flock of sheep, an enterprise which now yields the highest income per worker in this branch in Israel, and a feeding efficiency among the best in the country. Kibbutz Gevim had developed over 100 dunams of a flower and bulbs nursery that competes successfully on the international market with Dutch, Japanese, and American produce. Kibbutz Hefzibah made its fish ponds two meters deep, instead of one (the common practice), thereby saving land area and obtaining yields out of all proportion to the added investment, with the further advantage of deriving an extra water supply from saline streams and surplus sources. Kibbutz Ammiad received a prize for all-round inventiveness in farming.[2] A more recent report states that Kibbutz Yagur experimented with the use of recovered sewage water for fish ponds and found that this resulted not only in a saving of water, but also of fish fodder.[3]

PRODUCTIVITY IN AGRICULTURE, 1949–1960

For the twelve-year period, 1949–1960, Table 8 indicates an annual (compounded) rate of growth of 15.8 per cent in agricultural output; 2.1 per cent in the agricultural labor force; and 11.5 per cent in fixed reproducible agricultural assets of the kibbutzim. This would suggest that productivity increased at a very high rate of 10.1 per cent annually. During the latter half of the period 1955–1960, kibbutz agricultural production advanced at an average rate of 12.7 per cent; the agricultural labor force

TABLE 8. INDEX OF INPUT AND OUTPUT OF KIBBUTZ AGRICULTURE

YEAR	GROSS AGRICULTURAL OUTPUT IN 1949 PRICES	AGRICULTURAL LABOR FORCE	FIXED REPRODUCIBLE AGRICULTURAL ASSETS
1949	100	100	100
1950	132	103	126
1951	151	104	148
1952	193	106	163
1953	194	108	183
1954	233	118	206
1955	275	125	222
1956	325	125	242
1957	349	117	261
1958	401	126	289
1959	434	120	312
1960	500	125	330

Sources: Statistical Manuals; Statistical Abstracts of Israel; "Agricultural Production," Hakibbutz Hameuhad (June 1959) p. 4; *Economic Quarterly* (March 1963), p. 102.

showed very little change; and fixed reproducible capital in agriculture increased at an average 8.3 per cent annually. Productivity therefore increased at an annual average rate of 11.0 per cent for this six-year period, or about the same as for the twelve-year period as a whole. It is interesting to compare these results with those of Dr. A. L. Gaathon of the Research Department of the Bank of Israel.[4] His findings for Israeli agriculture as a whole for the period 1950–1959 show productivity of agriculture per unit of input increasing at a rate of 6.4 per cent annually (excluding irrigation assets); and for the period 1955–1959, at an annual average rate of 8.2 per cent (8.5 per cent including irrigation assets).

In kibbutz agriculture, productivity increased at an annual average rate of 11.3 per cent for the 1950–1959 period and 10.9 per cent for the 1955–1959 period.* Since the kibbutzim provided so large a part of Israel's agricultural output (between 27 per cent and 31 per cent), their exclusion from Gaathon's analysis of Israeli agriculture would undoubtedly have lowered the growth rates in productivity for the non-kibbutz agricultural sector and therefore increased the gap between the two sectors. It is significant that Gaathon found productivity increasing as the decade progressed, undoubtedly due to the fact that the very large number of new moshavim established during the first half of the 1950's were gaining experience and acquiring skills necessary for the operation of a farm. In the kibbutzim productivity increases during 1955–1960 are about the same as for the 1949–1960 period as a whole, reflecting the fact that the number of new kibbutzim was much smaller, since almost all of them had been settled by 1950 (there were 212 kibbutzim in 1950 and 225 listed by the Audit Union at the end of 1959). Another factor which has apparently raised productivity in the moshav sector since the mid-1950's is the exodus of the less successful moshav farmers to the cities and towns and the greater selectivity of the Jewish Agency's Settlement Department in choosing candidates for the moshav farms.

Another study made in 1960 showed that during the years 1953 to 1958 the kibbutz agricultural worker produced between 65 and 119 per cent more than the non-kibbutz Jewish agricultural worker.[5] The variations from year to year are largely a result of the periodic droughts which plague Israel, and since the kibbutz share of Israel's unirrigated field crops is so large, it is affected to a greater extent than the other sectors. Figures for 1959 show that the kibbutz agricultural worker produced 43 per cent more than the non-kibbutz Jewish agricultural worker and in 1960 about 74 per cent more. The reasons for the marked

* To make the comparison with Gaathon's findings, the same method of calculating productivity was used. The distributive national income shares of labor and capital were approximately 67% and 33%, respectively. Accordingly, total input was calculated by multiplying the index of labor change and the index of capital change by their respective weights. Productivity was then calculated by dividing the index of output change by the index of input change (less 100).

rise in 1960 seem to be the large drop in prices in poultry, and the hoof and mouth disease in the dairy branch, which affected the moshav sector much more than the kibbutz sector, since the former specializes in these two branches.

A study reported in the Economic Quarterly of Israel, relating to agriculture in the kibbutz and the moshav ovdim shows that the latter have increased agricultural production per worker to a far greater extent than the kibbutzim between the years 1957 and 1960. Thus the agricultural worker in the moshav ovdim produced approximately 53 per cent of his counterpart in the kibbutz in 1957, and 71 per cent in 1960.[6] This is further borne out by comparing labor productivity (rather than total productivity) of the kibbutz sector with Gaathon's findings for Israeli agriculture as a whole. For the twelve-year period 1949–1960, labor productivity (gross agricultural output per kibbutz agricultural worker) increased at an average rate of 13.4 per cent annually, and during the latter six years of this period at a slightly lower rate of 12.6 per cent. From 1950–1959 (for comparison with Gaathon's findings) labor productivity increased in the kibbutzim at an average annual rate of 12.2 per cent; in Israeli agriculture the rate was 7.3 per cent. However, during the latter part of the decade, 1955–1959, labor productivity in Israeli agriculture had shown a substantial increase, namely 10.8 per cent; in kibbutz agriculture it had risen by 13.2 per cent. If the rise in labor productivity of Israel agriculture during the latter part of the decade is compared to that in the first part (rather than to the average for the whole decade) an even greater increase can be noted in its rate of growth during the last five years of the decade as compared with the earlier period. This was due to the accumulation of experience and capital on the part of the moshav settlers who had begun their agricultural careers during the period of mass immigration and colonization following the independence of Israel.

Data are unfortunately unavailable with respect to total productivity for the individual branches of the kibbutz economy; instead, the yields and production per labor-day in a number of principal sectors of the collective economy will be considered.

Dairy Production. There are many factors affecting yields and labor productivity in the dairy branch. Smaller herds do not allow farmers to take advantage of economies of scale. Mechanization can, and has, substantially increased output per labor-day. Proper feeding methods can raise yields, and lower costs. With respect to economies of scale and mechanization, the kibbutzim possess a definite advantage vis-à-vis the small-scale moshav farmer. In terms of yields per cow the kibbutz sector has achieved much higher yields and increased these yields at a faster rate than the rest of Jewish agriculture (mainly the moshav sector). Thus, in 1953 the average yield per cow in the kibbutzim was 11 per cent higher than that in the other Jewish sectors of Israeli agriculture, and in 1959 it was 23 per cent higher. Yields per cow increased in the kibbutz during the above seven-year period at an average annual rate of 5.8 per cent; in the other sectors of Jewish agriculture the increase was at an average annual rate of 4.0 per cent.

Between 1959 and 1963 yields per cow increased at a much slower pace. The rate of increase in the non-collective Jewish sector was 1.4 per cent annually and in the kibbutz sector, 1.1 per cent. Nevertheless the gap between the two sectors remained very wide, approximately 22 per cent higher in the latter sector.[7] There is a definite trend in the moshav sector towards increasing specialization. The less successful (generally smaller) farmers are abandoning this branch and their quotas are being transferred by the moshav to the others. Profitable operation requires mechanization and this, in turn, presumes larger herds.

Table 9 indicates an average annual rate of growth in output per labor-day of 13.2 per cent in the dairy branch of the kibbutzim. This is substantially in keeping with the high growth rates

TABLE 9. LITRES OF MILK PER WORK-DAY IN KIBBUTZ DAIRYING

YEAR	OUTPUT	YEAR	OUTPUT
1949	129	1955	234
1950	140	1956	268
1951	160	1957	314
1952	146	1958	405
1953	152	1959	464
1954	175	1960	503

Source: Audit Union, *Yediot* (June 1955), p. 12; (November 1958), p. 1; (October 1961), p. 15; (July 1962), p. 9.

in the kibbutz agricultural economy as a whole. In the case of the dairying branch, the factors explaining the high growth rates in productivity are not only higher yields, improved techniques, and mechanization (mainly the introduction of the milking machine), but also the fact that the collectives were able to fill the barns which had been built for 60 or 80 cows. A study comparing the dairy branch in England in 1960 with that of the kibbutz, showed that yields per cow in the kibbutz were approximately 75 per cent greater, and that output per labor-day in the kibbutz was approximately double that of the English dairy farmer. The average herd in England in 1960 was 23 cows, much larger than that of the private Israeli farmer.[8] A study comparing output per labor-day in the kibbutz dairy branch with that in the United States in 1956 showed that the output per labor-day was about 40 per cent higher in the collectives, in that year. The 17 per cent annual average increase in output per work-day in the kibbutz dairy between 1956 and 1960 has most probably increased the gap since that time.[9]

Poultry Production. Poultry is another branch which is well developed in the collectives, although the moshav has increasingly dominated this branch since the mid-1950's. Thus the kibbutz share of laying hens in Jewish Israeli agriculture declined from 23 per cent in 1955 to 16 per cent in 1960, reflecting not only the increasing number of moshavim, but their increasing specialization in this branch (and to a lesser extent in the dairy branch). The extent of increasing specialization of the moshav sector in the poultry and dairy branches is shown by a survey of the Falk Project for Economic Research in Israel. The survey showed that in the well-established family farms in 1954 the poultry branch constituted 49 per cent of their total production and the dairy branch 36 per cent, the two branches combined providing 85 per cent of their gross output. By 1958, the poultry branch in these farms provided 56 per cent of total output, and the combined output of dairy and poultry was 92 per cent of total agricultural output of these farms.[10] However, the higher yields in the kibbutz sector make their position in this branch of agriculture of considerably greater importance than is reflected by their share of the number of laying hens in the country. Thus in 1955 when the kibbutz had 23 per cent of the total number of laying hens in the country, they produced 30 per cent of total egg production, and in 1959 when their share of laying hens had declined to 16 per cent, they provided 21.7 per cent of Israel's egg production. Furthermore, the quantities do not reflect their leading position in the provision of higher-priced eggs for hatcheries, and of day-old chicks.

Yields per laying hen have increased at a faster rate in the moshav farm as compared with the kibbutz during the period 1950–1959. Yields in the non-kibbutz Jewish agricultural sector increased at an average annual rate of 4.6 per cent as compared with 3.4 per cent in the collectives; but the gap between the kibbutz poultry branch and that in the rest of Jewish Israeli agriculture (mainly, the moshav) remained substantial. In 1959 the number of eggs per laying hen was about 25 per cent higher in the kibbutz sector. One reason for this differential is the much higher investment in the modern "American" type of chicken coop prevalent in the kibbutzim, costing about three times that of the simpler type of coops common to most moshav farms. The branch manager and staff of the poultry branch in the kibbutzim are constantly seeking and emulating advanced techniques. They are sent out for "extension" courses given by the Department of Agriculture or the Histadrut.

In terms of production per labor-day it is difficult to make comparisons with the moshav sector, since in the moshav substantial use is made of the wife's and children's labor in this branch. The Horowitz Committee Report states that in the large modern chicken coop, one worker is able to take care of about three times the number of chickens as compared with the intermediate or small coop prevalent in the moshav.[11] This, combined with the much higher yields in the collective sector, would give an indication of comparative outputs per labor-day.

Grains and Fruits. In the case of the wheat and barley crops which are generally unirrigated, there is an uneven pattern due primarily to the periodic droughts; but there is a definite downward trend in the number of labor-days required to produce a ton of product, i.e., increasing output per labor-day. (A metric ton is equivalent to 2,204 pounds.) The green fodder crops and potatoes are irrigated, and the upward trend in gross production per worker is not subject to the larger fluctuations of the unirrigated crops. Surveys on productivity in the potato crop are available for 1959 and 1960 as well, i.e., 4.8 and 4.5 labor-days per ton of product (see Table 10).[12] Production per agricultural worker in this branch has more than doubled over the twelve-year period surveyed. The wheat, barley, green fodder, and hay crops constituted 75 per cent of the total value of field crops in the collective settlements in 1958, and 77 per cent in 1959; and can therefore be considered representative of growth rates in production per worker for the field crops of the kibbutzim (other

TABLE 10. NUMBER OF LABOR-DAYS REQUIRED TO PRODUCE
ONE METRIC TON OF PRODUCT IN KIBBUTZIM (I)

YEAR	WHEAT	BARLEY	GREEN FODDER IRRIGATED	HAY	POTATOES
1949	4.6	3.3	1.4	2.2	9.3
1950	4.0	4.3	1.4	2.2	8.0
1951	5.6	3.6	1.0	2.7	7.3
1952	3.4	3.3	1.3	1.5	6.5
1953	4.9	3.3	1.2	1.5	7.5
1954	3.2	3.0	1.2	1.6	7.3
1955	4.2	2.9	1.0	1.9	5.7
1956	3.4	2.7	0.9	1.7	5.3
1957	2.7	2.1	0.8	1.7	5.0
1958	3.0	2.5	0.8	1.7	5.8

Sources: Audit Union, *Yediot*; Haim Darin-Drabkin, *The Other Society*
(Tel Aviv, 1961), p. 267.

than industrial crops). Industrial crops were introduced in Israel
in the mid-1950's and have become increasingly important to
Israel's agricultural economy. In this category the main crops are
cotton, sugar beets, and peanuts. In 1959, these three crops constituted 82 per cent of the total value of Israel's industrial crops,
and 86 per cent in 1960. Table 11 indicates the growth in labor
productivity in these crops in the collective economy.

TABLE 11. NUMBER OF LABOR-DAYS REQUIRED TO PRODUCE
ONE METRIC TON OF PRODUCT IN KIBBUTZIM (II)

YEAR	COTTON	SUGAR BEETS	PEANUTS
1956	39.1	3.0	19.2
1957	22.9	2.2	23.3
1958	27.5	1.8	16.6
1959	27.5	1.5	10.6
1960	17.3	2.0	9.6

Source: Audit Union, *Yediot* (July 1962), pp. 17, 18.

Here, too, the trend is towards rapid increases in labor productivity. Yields per dunam in sugar beets were 8 per cent
higher than in Jewish farming as a whole in 1958, and 10 per
cent higher in 1959. A survey made in 1961 by the Negev Extension Bureau of kibbutzim and moshavim in that area with respect
to peanut yields, found that the collective settlements had yields
exceeding 400 kilograms per dunam, as compared with an average
of 371 in the neighboring moshavim. Their explanation of the

lower moshav yields is that this was due to a lack of adequate "know-how" and sometimes because of planting in unsuitable soils.[13]

Work norms published in 1960 by the Joint Planning Center of the Government of Israel and the Jewish Agency make explicit recognition of the advantage which the collective settlements have with respect to economies of scale and the greater degree of specialization of their agricultural labor force.

In Table 12 the close correlation between the differential work norms and the degree of mechanization is evident. The unirrigated field crops, wheat and barley, are virtually a completely

TABLE 12. LABOR-DAYS REQUIRED PER DUNAM IN
THE COLLECTIVES AND IN FAMILY FARMS

CROP	COLLECTIVES	FAMILY FARMS
Unirrigated Field Crops		
Wheat or Barley	3.4	6.0
Irrigated Field Crops		
Cotton	68	85
Peanuts	36	46
Sugar beets	44	55
Sorghum	9	15
Vegetables		
Potatoes (spring)	74	95
Potatoes (fall)	58	80
Carrots (spring)	120	142
Onions (sown)	92	106
Cucumbers (spring)	160	175
Cucumbers (summer)	128	135
Watermelons	44	54

Source: Haim Darin-Drabkin, *The Other Society* (Tel Aviv, 1961), p. 277.

mechanized operation, and the advantage of large contiguous tracts of land is considerable. The Planning Center sets a 75 per cent higher labor norm for the small family farms. In the irrigated field crops, where there is a greater degree of manual labor, the advantage of the collective is generally smaller, though considerable. The same is true of the potato and watermelon crops where mechanical operations are possible for a considerable part of the work. With the other vegetable crops which require a considerable amount of manual labor, the advantage of the collective is minor. It is for this reason (as well as the surpluses of these crops, and the labor shortage in the kibbutzim) that the collective settlements have tended to abandon these crops to the moshav and Arab farmers.

In the case of banana plantations, no comparisons are possible with other agricultural sectors in Israel, since the kibbutzim effectively monopolize this branch in Israel. In 1959 they produced 87 per cent of Israel's banana crop. Audit Union surveys show that during the six-year period 1950–1955, yields averaged 1,190 kilograms per dunam and labor inputs, 15.6 labor-days per dunam, i.e., about 13 work-days per ton. In their surveys made each year from 1956 to 1960, they found that yields per dunam averaged 1,473 kilograms, an increase of 24 per cent, labor-days per dunam were 12.9 and therefore the labor-days required per ton of bananas had decreased to 11.1.[14]

PRODUCTIVITY IN AGRICULTURE, 1961–1964

Estimates for the kibbutz agricultural economy as a whole for the years 1961 and 1962 indicate a continuation of the high growth rates (about 10 per cent or 11 per cent in each year) somewhat less than the 12.7 per cent average growth rate maintained during the period 1955–1960. The corresponding rates for Israel's agricultural economy were 8.5 per cent in 1961 and 7 per cent in 1962.[15] Between 1959 and 1962, the agricultural labor force in Israel has been almost constant, rising by about 1 per cent in 1961 and declining by the same amount in 1962.[16] Thus the growth rate in agricultural production would parallel production per agricultural worker. In the agricultural economy of the collectives, the labor force surveys of the Central Bureau of Statistics show a decline of 14 per cent in 1961 (as compared with 1960), indicating that labor productivity increased considerably more than the 10 or 11 per cent rise in agricultural output in the collective settlements. Gross investment in farms (as distinct from investment by the government in country-wide irrigation projects) has been declining every year since 1957. The kibbutzim, which had been in many cases suffering financial difficulties (a subject of our next chapter on profitability) and a declining labor force, have not maintained the high rate of agricultural investment of the first decade after Israel's independence. The gains in agricultural production are largely in terms of total (factor) productivity.

The growth of agricultural output in the collectives in 1963 was possibly about 4 per cent. To some extent this was due to the partial drought, but the situation was offset by a considerable growth in meat and citrus production. In 1964 there was a very sharp rise in output, estimated at 16 to 17 per cent. This resulted from favorable weather conditions which brought bumper yields of field crops and fruit (other than citrus). The output of field crops increased by 30 per cent (including a 16 per cent increase in cotton), and of non-citrus fruits, 38 per cent. Since the kibbutzim dominate these branches in Israeli agriculture their growth rate exceeded that of other sectors.

Labor force summaries of Hakibbutz Ha'artzi Federation show a decline of over 4 per cent in labor inputs in agriculture in 1963, as compared with the previous year.[17] Since this federation constitutes over one-third of the total kibbutz population, it can probably be taken as representative of collective agriculture as a whole. This would indicate an increase of over 10 per cent in agricultural production per worker in 1963. In 1964 the federation had an increase of over 4 per cent in labor inputs in farming. Thus the growth in production per agricultural worker was over 12 per cent in 1964 (see Appendix X). Net investment in collective agriculture has generally been declining during the 1960's as compared with the rapid expansion typical of the prior decade (see Table 5, p. 43). It would seem, therefore, that the productivity of collective agriculture between 1960 and 1964 continued to increase at the same high rate which typified its performance in the 1950's.

While high rates of production in the collective settlements place them ahead of other sectors of Israeli agriculture, the same is not necessarily true in comparison with the American farmer. S. Baumgart of the Joint Planning Center of the Government of Israel and the Jewish Agency, studying eight various operations in sugar beets, cotton, tomatoes, and potatoes, found that in the productivity of manual labor, California farmers were far superior to the collective settlements. The collective farmer in Israel took about double the time required in California for similar tasks.[18]

In terms of international comparisons of gross agricultural output per persons employed in agriculture, the kibbutzim have reached a level, more or less, on a par with that of the western European countries,[19] but much lower than that of the United States. Their gross agricultural output per worker in 1961 was approximately one-half of the American average (the dairy branch is an exception to this generalization).[20]

Although the agricultural branches have been the mainstay of the economy of the large majority of kibbutzim, they have derived from a quarter to a third of their net income from non-agricultural sources. The percentage derived from outside work has been declining, while that derived from their industrial enterprises has been rising. Their non-agricultural economy has quite a complex structure: they are shareholders or partners in co-operative trucking firms, national bus cooperatives, industries owned by regional councils, and joint ventures with private capital. These are set up as separate firms, with their own management and bookkeeping. The kibbutz members in their employ receive wages and salaries, and the kibbutz receives a share of the distributed profits as well. The lack of data with respect to gross and net production of these firms, the kibbutz share of that production, and the kibbutz share of the labor force and capital assets, make a detailed analysis of productivity of these ventures virtually impossible. Furthermore, about half of the workers listed by the Central Bureau of Statistics as working in manufacturing and crafts in the collectives are estimated to be engaged in providing repair and other services mostly for the other branches of the collective economy. An estimate made by Darin-Drabkin indicated that in 1959 gross production per worker in industry and crafts in the collectives was approximately 84 per cent of the average for the country. Excluding those working in crafts (including only those that produce for the general market) he found that gross production per worker was approximately equivalent to that of the industrial worker in Israel. In terms of value-added in manufacturing, his estimate was that the kibbutz industrial worker was more productive. In terms of reproducible assets per worker, he found that the two sectors were about equal.[21]

While the kibbutz structure gives it certain advantages in the agricultural economy as compared with the small family farms prevalent in Israel, it has no such advantage with respect to industrial enterprises. The large industrial enterprises in Israel are privately owned or are Histadrut firms or State enterprises and the kibbutzim have neither the capital resources nor the labor force to attain the economies of scale of these firms. While Israel's agricultural economy is well protected by the government from the effects of foreign competition and is the recipient of many direct and indirect subsidies, this is much less true of the industrial sector. The government has already removed import restrictions on many industrial goods and plans to expand the list of such goods. All this does not mean that the industrial economy of the collectives will cease to expand, but that there are considerable obstacles facing the collectives in their drive towards further industrial expansion. On the other hand there are strong economic forces, primarily the poorer profitability of agriculture, pressing the collectives towards further industrial expansion. It would seem that the economic incentives which dictate greater emphasis on non-agricultural pursuits have thus far outweighed the non-economic factors, namely, the ideological opposition to hired labor.

VI

THE PROFITABILITY OF THE
KIBBUTZ ECONOMY

Despite the fact that profit maximization did not constitute the goal of the kibbutz, it has always been a prime tenet to be a self-sustaining economy; and to the extent that the desire for profits did not conflict with its ideology, the collectives have sought ways and means of increasing their profitability and the net worth of their economy. In reality, the financial difficulties which the kibbutzim faced throughout most of their history have provided a powerful incentive towards profit maximization. For example, in spite of the strong opposition of the movement to the use of hired labor, the economic managers have prevailed and the use of hired labor continues, especially in the industrial enterprises.

Until the mid-1930's, the kibbutzim generally failed to balance their budgets. The decade of the 1920's was one of severe deflation in Palestine, especially affecting the prices of agricultural goods, and the collectives suffered frequent losses. But the large-scale immigration of Jews from Nazi Germany, which began in 1933, brought about a period of prosperity and inflation. The depression of the 1930's in most of the Western countries, enabled the collectives to purchase agricultural equipment and other inputs at depressed prices, while prices of agricultural produce in the country were rising. The local inflation eased the repayment of past loans and the net worth of the older kibbutzim of that time showed a considerable increase in real terms. As a result the balance sheets of the established collectives showed a small profit of 1.8 Palestinian pounds per family unit in 1937; 33, in 1941 and a sharp decline after World War II to 2.5 Palestinian pounds in 1947. (The Palestinian pound was equivalent to the pound sterling.) [1]

In Chapter IV it was pointed out that the first five or six years following Israel's independence were very favorable to agricultural development: the new government provided protection from external competition, as well as considerable direct aid, to the agricultural settlements; mass immigration provided a seller's market for agricultural as well as industrial goods; and the very rapid inflation eroded the real burden of the debts. The accumulated experience and equipment of the older collectives enabled them to take full advantage of this situation. The balance sheets of the older settlements showed a profit of IL 67 per family unit in 1950. In 1952 the kibbutz balance sheets, as a whole, showed a profit per family unit of IL 88, IL 66 in 1953, and IL 58 in 1954. In real terms (correcting for price changes) the decline in reported profits is much sharper, namely, IL 88, 51, and 41 (in constant 1952 prices) in the years 1952 to 1954. In 1955 the kibbutzim indicated a loss of IL 72 in their income statements (or IL 48 in 1952 prices), and in 1956 they again show a profit of IL 78 per family unit (or IL 47 in 1952 prices).[2]

ANALYSIS OF PROFITABILITY

To analyze the meaning of the profits reported by the kibbutzim in their balance sheets and income statements, the concept of profit as the kibbutz defines it must be understood first; and secondly, the reliability or accuracy of their reported profits must be evaluated. Since the collective is a producing unit as well as a consuming unit, and the accounts are a composite of both sectors within the collective, the profit (or loss) is essentially equivalent to saving or dissaving. The kibbutz as a producing unit may be as profitable as any other unit of production, but if consumption increases either because of additional dependents, or because of higher living standards or higher living costs, the consolidated accounts will show a lesser profit or a loss. The converse is obviously equally true (conceptually), that kibbutz profits can be increased even when the income-producing branches are less efficient, through greater efficiency in the consumption branches or through lowering the standard of living.

Even using the kibbutz definition of profit, the accuracy of their reported profits and losses is open to serious doubt. The kibbutzim (like most firms) record the value of their assets in accordance with their historical value. In other words, the collective records the value of the assets as being the price actually paid for the purchase of the assets. Annual depreciation costs will therefore be some estimated percentage of the recorded value of the asset. In a country with constant prices, or at least, approximately so, this procedure would be valid. In Israel the inflation has been so great that the recorded value of assets, and therefore, depreciation allowances based on them, are meaningless. The rapid price rises of the 1930's and 1940's have already been pointed out in Chapter II. The investment price index in Israel showed an increase of 463 per cent in the twelve-year period 1950 to 1961 and following the devaluation of the Israeli pound in February 1962, there was a further sharp rise of 20 per cent for the year 1962, a total increase of 576 per cent during a thirteen-year period (see Appendix XI). During the latter half of the 1950's the annual increases in the investment price indexes became progressively smaller, from an increase of 6.3 per cent (as compared with the previous year) in 1957 to an increase of 1.0 per cent in 1959 and 4.2 per cent in 1960. Similarly the consumer price index showed very rapid increases, almost quadrupling over the thirteen-year period 1950–1962. These rapid increases in investment prices granted the kibbutzim (as well as any other investors in real assets) a "capital gain" in the form of an increasing net worth (the gap between the appreciating value of their assets and the depreciating value of their debts). At the same time it was incumbent upon them to set aside increasing depreciation allowances (in current Israeli pounds) to reflect the true costs of current production and to provide for the replacement of discarded assets. This they usually failed to do.

Kaddar's Analysis. Gershon Kaddar, the Agricultural Advisor of the Bank Leumi Le-Israel, the largest bank in the country, analyzed the balance sheets of the kibbutzim for the four-year period 1954–1957. He followed the kibbutz definition of profitability, i.e., the difference between total incomes, including both market sales and production for internal consumption, and total expenditures, corrected for realistic depreciation allowances. Ignoring the evaluation of assets as stated in the kibbutz accounts, he estimated that the real depreciation of assets was approximately equivalent to 10 per cent of their production in that year. This estimate was based on an evaluation of the Planning Division of Hakibbutz Ha'artzi Federation. He then took the annual figures for gross investment in fixed assets (in current Israeli pounds) and estimated additional investment in current assets during a

given year to be 30.5 per cent of gross investment in fixed assets.
He concluded that in each of the four years the kibbutzim, as a
whole, showed considerable net losses, as indicated in Table 13.
He concluded that, in effect, the kibbutzim were consuming their

TABLE 13. ESTIMATE OF KIBBUTZ LOSSES
(in millions of current Israeli pounds)

	YEAR			
	1954	1955	1956	1957
Gross investment in fixed assets	42.5	51.0	52.5	45.5
Gross investment in current assets	9.9	8.0	8.0	10.1
Total (additional) investment	52.5	59.0	60.5	55.6
Increase in total debt	43.0	54.0	63.0	38.0
Profit or loss before deduction of depreciation	9.4	5.0	−2.5	17.6
Depreciation allowances (est.)	13.0	15.5	18.1	21.5
Net loss	3.6	10.5	20.6	3.9

Source: Gershon Kaddar, "The Profitability in Agriculture," Bank Leumi
Le-Israel (April 1958), p. 12.

assets, which had been provided them by the government, the
Jewish Agency, and the other public bodies in Israel. Dividing
the 222 kibbutzim of that time into four groups, in accordance
with their age, he found that all groups, with the exception of the
oldest group (the 44 settlements established before 1935), had
suffered losses in 1957. In that year the "average" kibbutz in the
oldest group showed a profit of IL 34,000, compared with a loss
of IL 142,000 in the previous year and a loss of IL 31,000 in 1955.
All the other groups of kibbutzim showed consistent losses
during the period surveyed. He further estimated the amounts
received from direct subsidies to agricultural produce provided
by the government (and by the Jewish Agency as well) to the
younger kibbutzim and moshavim, and found that the profits of
the oldest group of kibbutzim in 1957 were attributable to subsidies (profits for the average kibbutz in the oldest grouping were
IL 34,000, while direct subsidies received were IL 36,600). Losses
without subsidies in the other groupings would have doubled.[3]

The appearance of this publication in 1958 created quite a stir
in Israel, and many articles appeared in various journals challeng-
ing the validity of his estimates. The main criticisms were levelled

at Kaddar's estimates for "additional investment in current assets" based on a fixed ratio of 30.5 per cent of gross investment in fixed assets, and secondly at his estimate for depreciation allowances based on 10 per cent of current gross production. As the first years after independence were a period of strict rationing of feed supplies, fertilizers, and other goods, and restricted allocations of spare parts, building materials, and many other things, the kibbutzim, as well as other producers, were anxious to keep large stores of these supplies. As controls were relaxed, and supplies became more plentiful, all producers would have every incentive to reduce inventories. There would therefore be no justification in assuming that the ratio between fixed and current assets obtaining in the early 1950's should be applicable to the 1954–1957 period under study. Furthermore, the estimate for depreciation of fixed assets based on current gross production may have been approximated in certain years, but economic reasoning provides no basis for assuming that this was anything but fortuitous, and consequently provides no basis for future estimates of realistic depreciation allowances.

Lowe's Analysis. Dr. Yehuda Lowe used another approach in estimating the profitability of the kibbutzim (using their definition of profitability). His estimate for the real evaluation of fixed assets per agricultural worker in the collective is based on sampling done by the Planning Division of the Ministry of Agriculture with respect to the various agricultural branches. He estimated that, based on historical experience, the investment per worker in industry was half of that required for the agricultural worker. The number of family units occupied in agriculture, industry, and outside work (the latter requires no investment in productive assets within the kibbutz) was taken from the reports of the Audit Union. He included, as did Kaddar, investment in housing as well as other consumer fixed assets. His estimate for annual depreciation allowances (based on the Planning Division's data) was 5 per cent of the real evaluation of fixed assets. The results for each of the four groupings of kibbutzim are shown in Table 14.

According to Lowe's estimates all the groups of kibbutzim incurred losses in each of the three years, though considerably less than those shown in Kaddar's estimates. His estimate for 1954 losses of all the kibbutzim was IL 2.8 million (compared with Kaddar's IL 3.6 million); in 1955, IL 5.5 million (compared with Kaddar's IL 10.5 million); and in 1956, IL 5.3 million (compared

TABLE 14. LOSSES PER KIBBUTZ FAMILY UNIT
(in current Israeli pounds)

Kibbutzim Established Before 1935	1954	1955	1956
Profits per family unit before deduction of depreciation	680	660	685
Depreciation in terms of reproduction value of assets (est.)	800	880	950
Net loss per family unit	120	220	265
Kibbutzim Established 1936–1943			
Profits per family unit before deduction of depreciation	540	525	630
Depreciation in terms of reproduction value of assets (est.)	730	820	900
Net loss per family unit	190	295	270
Kibbutzim Established 1944–1947			
Profits per family unit before deduction of depreciation	440	445	580
Depreciation in terms of reproduction value of assets (est.)	650	740	820
Net loss per family unit	210	295	240
Kibbutzim Established Since 1948			
Profits per family unit before deduction of depreciation	440	170	380
Depreciation in terms of reproduction value of assets (est.)	600	650	780
Net loss per family unit	160	480	400

Source: Y. Lowe, "The Problems of Kibbutz Profitability," Ministry of Agriculture (Tel Aviv, 1959), p. 10.

with Kaddar's IL 20.6 million). Following Lowe's estimate of annual 5 per cent depreciation of all fixed assets, it would seem that the losses in the kibbutzim in 1957 were approximately IL 3 million (compared with Kaddar's IL 3.9 million). Though Lowe's estimates of losses of the kibbutzim are considerably lower than Kaddar's, he arrives at the same general conclusion, namely, that the kibbutzim during this period were currently consuming more than their current net income. Moreover, the analysis shows that these losses applied to the older kibbutzim as well as to the relatively younger ones. It should be emphasized that even these estimates for the "average" kibbutz within each group are not equally applicable to all the settlements within the group. There were undoubtedly a number of collectives which did succeed in balancing their budgets and even showed net profits, but the data suggest that most kibbutzim suffered net losses during these years.

Losses in the Kibbutzim

Generally speaking, the trend indicates smaller losses per family unit in the oldest group of kibbutzim, though it is obvious that age is not the only factor. Those in the middle grouping had, during these years, the largest number of dependents per family unit, thus raising their consumption expenditures (i.e., their labor costs). The large decline in profits before deduction of depreciation in the youngest group in 1955 is due to the drought in the southern Negev, where many of them are located. The variations in year to year incomes are, therefore, less pronounced in the older kibbutzim, since they had intensified their agriculture to a greater degree than their younger counterparts, and are less susceptible to the vagaries of the weather. They are also more industrialized, so that the wide fluctuations of agricultural production and prices affect them to a lesser extent. No doubt the factor of skills and experience is also present, though the gap between the older and younger kibbutzim, in this respect, generally narrows over time.

To keep the losses of the kibbutzim in proper perspective, they must be related to the total real value of their assets, and the total value of production. Even in the worst year, 1955 (in Lowe's survey), the loss per family unit was about 1.9 per cent of the real value of fixed assets per family unit (and a smaller percentage of total assets), and 3.8 per cent of total gross production. This would seem to suggest that with slightly better management of the productive branches and greater efficiency in the consumption branches, it might well have been possible to erase, or at least reduce, the deficit.

A more recent study of 113 established kibbutzim comparing their financial position in 1959 with that existing in those settlements in 1954, would lead to similar conclusions. These collectives represent about half the number in the country and were all established before 1948. In terms of population and incomes they represent the bulk of the kibbutz movement. Table 15 indicates that during the five-year period their total assets (as stated in the balance sheets) increased by IL 157 million, and their total liabilities by IL 147 million. The understatement of the real value of fixed assets is undoubtedly greater in the older kibbutzim, where a considerable part of total investment had taken place at much lower prices. The net income of these settlements (before deduc-

TABLE 15. FINANCIAL SITUATION OF 113 ESTABLISHED KIBBUTZIM
(in millions of current Israeli pounds)

	1955	1959
Fixed assets	100	214
Total assets	130	287
Total liabilities	122	269
Total income	113	189
Interest payments	7.2	19.1
Interest payments as per cent of income	6.3	10.1

Source: S. Rosen, "An Uncompleted Mission," Al Hamishmar, April 22, 1960, p. 2.

tion of interest charges and depreciation allowances) was IL 30 million in 1959. Interest payments in that year amounted to IL 19 million, leaving a net profit, before depreciation allowances, of IL 11 million. Fixed assets, as stated in the balance sheets were IL 214 million. Lowe's estimates of the real value of fixed assets in *all* the kibbutzim in 1955 is approximately double their "book" value, and the under-evaluation is greatest in the older settlements. Even with a very conservative estimate of the true valuation of fixed assets in the established kibbutzim in 1959 as being 50 per cent higher than their "book" value and Lowe's estimate of 5 per cent depreciation allowances, net losses in these kibbutzim would total IL 5 million in 1959.

Calculating the real evaluation of fixed assets of the collectives in the years 1958 to 1962 on the basis of net investment in each and revalued in accordance with the investment price index, and using Lowe's estimate of annual 5 per cent depreciation allowances, it would appear that the kibbutzim as a whole showed a net loss of IL 6 million in 1958, a loss of IL 10 million in 1959, a loss of IL 3 million in 1960, a surplus of IL 10 million in 1961, and based on preliminary estimates, a surplus of IL 8 million in 1962. It may very well be that, as a result of a greater percentage of gross investment in the kibbutzim (as well as other agricultural sectors) going into mechanical equipment, compared with the greater emphasis on investment in land and buildings in the earlier period, the use of a 5 per cent annual depreciation allowance with respect to total fixed assets may understate the real depreciation of assets in recent years. In any case, the conclusion would still be the same, i.e., that the kibbutzim, *as a whole*, suffered net losses (or net dissaving) during the period 1954 to 1960, and then showed net profits in 1961 and 1962. What is probably more important, the analysis seems to indicate that losses during the above-mentioned seven-year period were quite widespread, encompassing in many, if not most, of these years, the older as well as the younger settlements. It is true that the net worth (total assets minus total liabilities) increased by about 50 per cent between 1954 and 1961 (in current Israeli pounds) and increased very considerably in 1962 as a result of the devaluation, but this "capital gain" must be attributed to inflation rather than to profitability and net saving.

Further corroboration of deficits in 1959 and smaller losses in 1960 is found in a report of Hakibbutz Ha'artzi regarding its member kibbutzim. The report [4] stated that 35 of the 73 member kibbutzim of the federation showed a profit; 20 settlements just covered depreciation; 17 did not manage to show a sufficient balance in their accounts to cover depreciation allowances. Since the balance sheets allow for depreciation in accordance with the historical costs of fixed assets, it is quite evident that the majority of their settlements incurred deficits. It is also probable that the 35 settlements which reported profits include a large majority of the older well-established collectives, in which the under-evaluation of assets is greatest, since a major part of their investment had taken place at much lower investment prices. It will be recalled that Lowe's estimate of the real evaluation of fixed assets of all the kibbutzim in 1955 was about double their stated value in the balance sheets; in the older kibbutzim the discrepancy was much greater. Obviously, even some of the 35 (out of 73) kibbutzim with reported profits had real deficits. The report further states (without elaboration) that 1960 was an improvement over 1959, indicating that an even larger number of settlements had incurred losses in 1959. It seems probable that the profitability of the kibbutzim of Hakibbutz Ha'artzi Federation (one-third of the kibbutz movement) reflects the position of the kibbutz movement, as a whole.

CAUSES FOR DEFICITS

The question now arises regarding the causes for the deficits of the kibbutzim during the period 1954 to 1960, and what factors might explain the surpluses shown in 1961 and 1962. Accepting the premise that the kibbutz is not a profit-maximizing organization, an explanation for its failure to balance its budget over an extended period must still be sought. Are the causes for this failure exogenous to the collective structure, from which it might be concluded that the removal of these external causes would restore the viability of the kibbutz economy, or are they inherent in the structure itself?

When the studies mentioned earlier appeared in Israel, indicating that the kibbutzim were, in effect, consuming annually part of the assets which they had acquired mainly through non-commercial loans of the Jewish Agency and through governmental loans, some writers concluded that the losses were attributable to the inherent structure of the kibbutz. As proof they compared the losses of the older kibbutzim with the profitability of the established moshavim and of the large administered farms in Israel, generally owned and operated by some units of the Histadrut. The large administered farms cultivate large tracts of land, using heavy equipment, comparable in these respects with the operation of the collective economy. They employ skilled managers as well as other skilled and unskilled personnel in accordance with seasonal labor requirements. These administered farms have shown profits at the same time that the kibbutzim have been incurring losses.[5]

To compare the two economies, the kibbutzim and the administered farms, similar standards must be applied. The kibbutz does not pay its members directly; it provides for them and their dependents not only on a year-round basis (without regard to seasonal labor requirements), regardless of their state of health, and the number of dependents, but also on a life-time basis, if they elect to remain in the settlement. The administered farm hires the employee only when it finds his employment profitable and then pays him the market wage. To compute what is equivalent to the wage cost in a kibbutz one would have to divide the total consumption costs by the number of workers in the income-producing branches. The kibbutz accounts do not provide a complete picture of consumption costs. The Audit Union accounts list five broad categories of expenditures: (1) direct costs of consumption, including home-produced goods; (2) direct costs of production, such as seeds, fertilizers, spare parts, etc.; (3) total interest paid during the year; (4) administrative and municipal expenditures; and (5) depreciation allowances. Labor-days in the various branches are listed separately. The unrealistic estimates for depreciation have already been discussed, but actually part of the interest costs, administrative and municipal costs, and (corrected) depreciation allowances should also be attributed to consumption expenditures. Dr. Lowe in his estimates of kibbutz losses in 1954, 1955, and 1956 made a separate estimate for the permanent membership of the collective, treating the many temporary workers (Youth Aliyah groups, Nahal groups, and others) as "hired workers" and deducting their costs of upkeep from the consumption expenditures of the kibbutz members and their dependents.

To these consumption expenditures of the family units we have added a (conservative) estimate of that part of interest costs, administrative expenditures, and depreciation allowances which are, in reality, consumption expenditures. This would add an average of 15 per cent to Lowe's calculation of direct consumption costs of the membership. The Audit Union Report (December 1957) indicates that about 48 per cent of the total labor-days of the kibbutz membership was in income-producing work. Accordingly, each member working in the income-producing branches "cost" the settlement IL 2,400 in 1954; IL 2,700 in 1955; and IL 3,000 in 1956. Since most of the members are in the skilled category in their various occupations we have selected the market wage rates of the skilled categories of workers for comparative purposes (as listed in the annual Statistical Abstracts of Israel). (The fact that 16 per cent of the labor-days in the income-producing branches were in the more-highly-paid wage categories of industry would certainly be offset by the fact that the market would not classify all other kibbutz members in the income-producing branches in the skilled or highly skilled agricultural categories.)

We have estimated the market daily wage of the kibbutz member as equivalent to IL 7.0 in 1954, IL 7.4 in 1955, and IL 8.1 in 1956. Assuming that the kibbutz member works 275 days per year, one would find that the income-producing branches "paid" the equivalent of IL 475 more than the equivalent market wage in 1954; IL 665 in 1955 and IL 770 in 1956. A brief glance at Lowe's estimates of kibbutz deficits in these three years would indicate that in each of the years surveyed, the kibbutzim in *all* categories would have shown surpluses, rather than deficits had their consumption costs (i.e., labor costs) been no greater than market wages. A survey of established family farms conducted by the Falk Project for Economic Research in Israel,[6] uses an estimate of IL 5.5 for per day imputed labor costs of the farm owner and his family. Had we used this figure for alternative wage costs in the kibbutz income-producing branches, instead of IL 7.0 daily wage used in the above estimate, this would put their labor costs 59 per cent above the market wage in 1954 (instead of the 25 per cent differential indicated in our estimates).

CONSUMPTION AND PRODUCTION

The conclusion indicated in the above analysis would be further strengthened by an understanding of the definition "income-producing" work in the collective. The kibbutz accounts define administrative work as being in the income-producing category. The rationale is that this would be equivalent to the administrative staff within any enterprise. While this is generally true, there is no doubt that a fraction of the time of the bookkeepers, labor manager, Secretariat, purchasing manager, internal secretary, and others is occupied with work that should be categorized as consumption, rather than production. Since this category occupied about 16 per cent of the total labor input in the "income-producing" classification, an estimate of even one-tenth of these labor-days within the non-income producing classification would further increase the labor costs of the income-producing branches, and increase the differential between these, and the alternative wage costs.

This analysis would seem to indicate that a prime factor explaining the poor profitability of the kibbutzim must be sought in the area of collective consumption, rather than of collective production. Until the 1950's the living standards in the kibbutzim were generally much lower than that of the urban worker with equivalent skills, or of the moshav farmer with similar capitalization and experience. The drive within the collectives during the 1950's to raise their previously low living levels has concurrently lowered their profitability. Their claims have been previously cited that by the end of the 1950's their living standards were not only equivalent to that of the average urban wage-earner, but were even on a par with the consumption standards of the better-paid Jewish immigrant from Europe.

Consumption Norms. It seems that the level of consumption within the collective is not determined primarily by the success or failure of its economy (as is generally the case in the private sector), but is a relatively independent factor determined by the "consumption norms" set by the kibbutz federations. These norms are published periodically and serve as a guide for the expenditures in money and in labor-days on various items such as food, clothing, etc. The only differentials are for the various age-groupings of settlements, and even here the differences are relatively minor, insofar as expenditures per member and per child are concerned. The membership, and particularly the heads of the various consumption branches and committees, expect and *demand* the provision of money and labor-days according to the norms, or more, and the treasurer and economic manager and labor manager are under constant pressure to meet these demands. The excessive employment of workers in the consumption branches, due to the fact that these norms serve as *universal* guides, and sometimes due to inefficiency of management, increases the amount of net income which those occupied in the income-producing branches must earn to balance the budget. The higher cash expenditures partially induced by these norms, further increases the net income which the income-producing branches must earn. Thus, the high standard of living instead of being dependent upon the total profitability of the collective economy is a relatively independent factor, determining the high cost of the labor force, and the resulting poor profitability of the collectives.[7]

Lowe, in his analysis of kibbutz losses, found that most of the losses the settlements incurred were due to a real rise in living standards. He calculated the extent of the losses which would have been incurred had the kibbutzim increased expenditures per adult and per child only in accordance with the rising consumer price index (Table 16).

For the kibbutzim as a whole, the real loss per family unit would have been IL 49 instead of IL 160 in 1954, and IL 117 instead of IL 300 in 1955. He concluded that these deficits are so small in relation to gross income per family unit per year, that one may safely assume that even minor improvements in management of the production and consumption branches would have erased these losses. One of the more serious problems for management is that it is not aware of the degree of profitability of current operations for six to twelve months after the close of the fiscal year, by which time conditions have frequently changed. By way of contrast, the wage or salary earner is very much aware of his current income and adjusts his current consumption expenditures accordingly. Even the small entrepreneur has a much clearer concept of current profitability of the firm than has the kibbutz management.

TABLE 16. EXTENT OF KIBBUTZ LOSSES PER FAMILY UNIT
DUE TO RISING LIVING STANDARDS
(in current Israeli pounds)

	KIBBUTZIM ESTABLISHED			
1954	Before 1935	1936–1943	1944–1947	Since 1948
Real loss	120	190	210	160
Rise in living standards	26	100	165	253
Loss without rise in living standards	94	90	45 (profit)	93
1955				
Real loss	220	296	295	480
Rise in living standards	184	265	99	120
Loss without rise in living standards	36	30	196	360

Source: Y. Lowe, "The Problems of Kibbutz Profitability" Ministry of Agriculture (Tel Aviv, 1959), p. 14.

Labor Force. What is probably more significant in terms of real costs is the fact that in three out of the four kibbutz groupings the percentage of the labor force in the income-producing branches declined significantly. The only group that shows a rise in the percentage employed in the income-producing branches is the group of kibbutzim established before 1935. Even here the change is very slight, from 47.3 per cent in 1951 to 47.7 per cent in 1955. In the group of kibbutzim established between 1936 and 1943 the percentage declined from 47.0 per cent to 45.7 per cent; in the group established between 1944 and 1947, the percentage declined from 51.7 per cent to 48.3 per cent and in the youngest group of kibbutzim, those established since 1948, the percentage in the income-producing branches declined from 55.7 per cent to 50.9 per cent.[8] The rising percentage of workers in the non-income-producing branches is undoubtedly partly a result of the rising number of children, but the Audit Union report indicates that services to adults increased, percentage-wise, more than the increase in the number of adults to be served. This would further strengthen our conclusion that the poor profitability of the kibbutzim was significantly affected by the consumption branches.

For the kibbutz movement, as a whole, the percentage of workers in the income-producing branches declined from 48.9 per cent in 1953 to 47.8 per cent in 1955.

The labor force summaries of Hakibbutz Ha'artzi Federation for 1956 to 1959 indicate that the percentage of workers in the income-producing branches was 46.6 per cent in 1956; 45.2 per cent in 1957; 44.3 per cent in 1958 and 44.7 per cent in 1959.[9] Recent data of this federation for the years 1960 to 1964 show that the percentage of kibbutz workers classified as income-producing has remained quite constant since 1959.[10] Certainly the downward trend in the percentage occupied in the income-producing branches in the collectives during the 1950's would be very significant in explaining the poor profitability of the kibbutzim during this period. This would go a long way towards clarifying the high productivity rates in the kibbutzim concomitant with poor profitability. Productivity rates are based on the income-producing branches, and these have been highly productive; profitability is a composite of the total collective economy. The lower the percentage of the population working in the income-producing branches, the more difficult it becomes to support the settlement. The higher the consumption expenditures, whether as a result of increased number of children or higher per capita consumption (or both), the higher the labor costs in the income-producing branches, and the more difficult it becomes to balance the kibbutz budget.

Comparison of Kibbutz and Moshav Profitability

It is instructive to compare the labor costs of the collective with those of the moshav family farm. In the kibbutz, the average adult member works 260–270 days per year. The other days comprise the Sabbaths, holidays, illness, and annual vacations. The collective prides itself that it affords its membership more leisure than the average farmer allows himself. There is an annual two-week vacation, plus special consideration for the older members and those who are physically weaker. It provides the women with a much lighter work-load during pregnancy, six weeks of complete rest after childbirth, with limited work-requirements for a number of months thereafter. In the moshav the average is 310 labor-days per year. This differential alone accounts for 18 per cent more labor input in the moshav as compared with the collective.

However, the structure of the kibbutz requires many more labor-days in the consumption branches, primarily in child care, than in the private family setup.

Comparing the established moshav with the established kibbutz, Lowe found that in the kibbutz the number of days occupied per family-unit for services to adults and children was 256; in the moshav, 218. Part of this difference is due to the fact that the moshav family purchases some of the services, such as education, repairs, and so on, while in the kibbutz these are usually provided by the members (although many, if not most, employ hired labor to provide some of these services to the extent that sufficient skilled manpower is lacking in these areas). He also estimated that the children in the moshav provide 47 per cent more labor-days than their counterparts in the kibbutz. This is partly accounted for by the fact that the kibbutzim provide a high school education for all their children, which is not equally true in the family farm.

Income-producing Units. Lowe's summaries indicate that in terms of income-producing work the moshav farm family provides 47 per cent more man-days than the equivalent kibbutz family.[11] A survey of the Falk Project for Economic Research in Israel found that in the average established family farm the family labor input in the farm was 450 work-days annually, consisting of 310 on the part of the farmer himself and 140 on the part of his wife and children. The Horowitz Committee Report considers the labor-day of the farmer's wife as equivalent to four-fifths of that of the farmer, and the child's work-day as equivalent to three-fifths.[12]

Since very few women in the collectives work in the income-producing branches, "corrections" for family labor, largely in the case of the moshav, should be made. Even after corrections, it would appear that the labor input in terms of man-days is at least 35 per cent higher in the moshav, insofar as work in the income-producing branches is concerned. Since these organizations differ so radically, all comparisons must be viewed with caution, but the general conclusion seems to be that the labor input in the moshav is considerably higher.

It is even more difficult to compare the collective organization with the private urban family. Nevertheless, the increasing trend visible in Israel, and in other countries, of wives and mothers going into the labor market, for part-time or full-time work, would also indicate that in terms of total labor inputs per family in income-producing work, the kibbutz suffers a distinct disadvantage. True, the working mother purchases more services than she would otherwise, but it must be presumed that the sum total of these increased services is less than her equivalent production and income.

Some argue that the above comparison between labor-inputs in the kibbutz and the moshav understates the differences between the two organizations. The moshav farmer, it is noted, like farmers everywhere, works more than the eight or nine-hour work-day (depending on the season) prevalent in the collective. Although his work-day may be an hour or two longer, it does not necessarily follow that actual work time is greater per day in the moshav, since the private farmer will spend considerable time going from one branch of his farm to another, whereas the kibbutz member is generally occupied in one particular branch. Even those few kibbutz members who have not acquired a special skill, and are shifted from job to job, are usually assigned to one particular branch for a full day's work. However, since the moshav farmer has more and more tended to specialize in the dairy and poultry branches, which are located near his home, it may very well be that the moshav farmer's daily labor input is greater than that of the kibbutz member (in addition to the much greater input in terms of labor-days). It is interesting, in this regard, to note that the average work-day of the American farm operator in 1959 was 10.6 hours, and for the farm employee, 9.3 hours.[13]

Even within the kibbutz movement itself there are considerable differences between one kibbutz and another with respect to the percentage of total labor-days in the income-producing branches. In fact, in the smaller kibbutzim (generally the younger ones) the structure of the collective requires a disproportionately large percentage of manpower in personal services and administrative staff. It was estimated that in Hakibbutz Hameuhad Federation in 1959, 14 per cent of the settlements had less than 45 per cent of the labor force in income-producing work, and this category, it will be remembered, includes the administrative staff. In over 20 per cent of the kibbutzim, more than 20 per cent of the "income-producing" labor force were in the administrative staff. One can assume that this situation paralleled that of the other federations as well. This puts a very heavy burden on the income-producing branches to carry, so to speak, large fixed labor costs.[14]

Within the existing setup, the kibbutz leaders realize that there is both waste and inefficiency, especially in the consumption branches, and they have enlisted the aid of the Productivity Institute of Israel to suggest ways and means of improvement.[15]

It is the opinion of Western observers that agriculture in the Western developed countries, based on the family farm and private enterprise, is more efficient than the kolkhoz farms in the Soviet Union. This is attributed, at least partially, to the factor of incentives. On the other hand, it must be emphasized that the kibbutz is a voluntary organization and therefore the incentives of the kibbutz member may differ radically from those of the kolkhoz farmer. Nevertheless, it may very well be that the profit-seeking moshav farmer's greater profitability is due, in part, to his desire to maximize profits.

Shift to Profitable Branches. This would explain the fact that since the mid-1950's the moshav farms have shifted their resources very rapidly into the more lucrative livestock branches. Between 1955 and 1959 the number of cattle (dairy and beef cattle) in the kibbutz sector increased by 70 per cent; in the rest of Jewish agriculture (mainly moshav) the increase was 138 per cent. Similarly, the number of laying hens increased in the kibbutz by 47 per cent; in the rest of Jewish agriculture by 128 per cent. Even if one considers the fact that the number of Jews engaged in agriculture outside the kibbutzim increased by 15 per cent, while the number engaged in agriculture in the collectives declined by 4 per cent during this period, the difference would still be considerable. In the non-kibbutz Jewish agricultural sectors the number of cattle per agricultural worker increased by 108 per cent; in the kibbutz sector, 77 per cent. In poultry, the number of laying hens per kibbutz agricultural worker increased by 53 per cent; in the rest of Jewish agriculture the increase was 100 per cent. The more rapid shift of resources in the moshavim towards the more profitable branches would provide an important element in explaining their greater profitability. A survey of established family farms showed an average net profit of IL 2,375 in 1954. Those moshav farms defined as "diversified" had a net profit of IL 984. It was by far the lowest of all the types of family farms.[16] Another study pertaining to the new moshav farms (those established since 1948) found that the net income in 1957 of those specializing in dairy was IL 3,006, and in the farms based on field crops, IL 1,768.[17] Of course, when the rapid expansion of livestock culminated in sharp price declines in 1959, the older moshavim were much more affected than the kibbutzim and other agricultural sectors that had not become so specialized. Even then the decline in net incomes in the older moshavim was from a much higher level of net incomes and was considerably alleviated by government subsidies.

Diversified Economy. Besides the decline in the income-producing units and the failure to shift to more profitable branches, another factor which might explain the generally poorer profitability of the kibbutzim is their adoption of the concept of a diversified economy. The rationale was the avoidance of wide fluctuations in production, income, and labor requirements which typify a monocultural economy. However, the goal of a diversified economy often runs counter to the maximization of profits, and will frequently bring about lower average net incomes than those obtainable through specialization. Immediately upon its establishment, each new collective would embark upon the development of all or most of the branches of a large, mature economy, to the detriment of profitable enterprise for many years. Indeed, this was in keeping with the policy of the Settlement Department of the Jewish Agency, recently reversed by the director of that department.

The result of this policy was that for many years each branch was unprofitable because of its small scale. The settlement would, for example, build a large barn for sixty or eighty head of cattle, without the necessary financing to fill that barn for the next five or eight years. Meanwhile, productivity was lower because of the small scale of operations, and the kibbutz had to bear the cost of financing and of depreciation of a large building. Similar examples could be cited for the other branches. The desire to expand the herd at a faster rate than that provided for by the limited and delayed budgets of the Jewish Agency, induced them to enter the private money market where interest rates were high, and the terms of payment totally unsuitable to the investment objective. The deteriorating financial position of these kibbutzim induced them to seek the development of such branches which, the experience of the older kibbutzim showed, yielded higher than average incomes. This further diversification and the resulting worsening of their debt structure, however, made their financial position even more precarious.[18]

On page 104, the survey cited there [19] indicated that among the moshav farms the lowest net incomes were in those classed as diversified. It is obvious that the much larger kibbutz economy would permit more diversification concurrent with large-scale branches. However, in the smaller, younger kibbutzim, given the large "overhead" in terms of the service and administrative branches, a multiplicity of branches must necessarily lead to lower incomes than would be obtainable with fewer large-scale branches. Of course, the collectives founded after independence (as well as a number of those initiated shortly before) anticipated that they would develop and grow in the same manner as their predecessors. No one foresaw, at that time, the much diminished attraction of the kibbutz movement since 1948.

Hired Labor. It must be emphasized again that the lack of manpower in many kibbutzim and their opposition to the use of hired labor are serious constraints in terms of full exploitation of their land and capital resources, and increase the percentage of members who must be engaged in the consumption branches and in administration, all of which has an adverse effect on their profitability. Dr. Sadan, an economist in the Faculty of Agriculture at the Hebrew University, has recently made (in the older kibbutzim) an estimate of the cost involved in their refusal to hire labor. He calculated the marginal productivity of the kibbutz agricultural worker and found that it was considerably higher than the market wage (as determined by the Histadrut). Thus, an addition to the labor force to the point where marginal productivity equals market wages would have increased the net incomes of the collectives (though lowering the high average productivities cited in the previous chapter). This bears out the contention of the government leaders that the refusal of the kibbutzim to hire labor, during the decade of the 1950's when Israel's unemployment rates were high, caused a net loss to the national economy (as well as lower profitability in the kibbutzim).[20] In a subsequent rebuttal,[21] Yosef Shatil disputed this contention, arguing that there are cogent economic as well as non-economic reasons justifying the opposition of the collectives to the employment of hired labor. It would seem to this writer that even if Sadan has exaggerated the extent of the loss incurred by the kibbutzim as a result of their ideology, his basic argument is valid. However, as Shatil implies, if the kibbutzim had employed hired labor on a much larger scale than they did, the effect upon the kibbutz members and the younger generation, *in the long run*, might well have caused widespread disillusionment within the settlements, and more defections than actually took place. The effect upon the affiliated youth organization in Israel and abroad could have been catastrophic, leaving the kibbutzim with few, if any, reinforcements to their ranks. The economic effects of such an eventuality are obvious.

Additional Causes for Kibbutz Unprofitability

There are a number of basic factors which have had, and continue to have, a negative *cumulative* effect upon the profitability of many kibbutzim. When the collectives chose a location for settlement, or agreed to the site offered them by the settlement authorities, the prime criterion was not the economic potential of the location; political and military considerations were paramount. The wave of new settlement which took place during the war of independence and immediately following the cessation of hostilities, was also considered a political and military act designed to ensure and strengthen the new State. In addition, the municipal expenditures including defense, education, health, and other minor items were very high. The estimate for total municipal expenditures in 1959 was between IL 500 and IL 600 per family unit.[22]

Municipal Expenditures. As the bulk of the new settlements was in the arid Negev, many kibbutzim suffered, and still do, handicaps of higher security costs (in addition to those paid for by the government); higher costs of water, even after the lengthy delays in making adequate water supplies available to them; greater distances from the markets, entailing greater direct transportation costs as well as indirect costs in terms of labor-days; and of course periodic droughts. Some of these costs are partially compensated by government and Jewish Agency direct and indirect subsidies. These subsidies do not, however, make them self-sustaining viable communities. Even assuming that the security costs have declined (relatively) since 1956, the per capita municipal expenditures (not reimbursed by the government) were far greater in the collective settlements in 1959 than in the other settlements.

The Horowitz Committee Report[23] estimated that security costs in the kibbutzim (after deducting those paid for by the government) in 1954 were IL 21 per capita. A less reliable estimate for the moshavim stated that their security costs were IL 3.5 per capita. Even granting the possibility of underestima-

tion in the case of the moshavim there is no doubt that the difference is considerable. The costs were especially heavy in the
younger kibbutzim. The collectives founded after Israel's independence incurred defense costs which averaged IL 46.8 per
capita in 1954; in the oldest group of kibbutzim the per capita
average cost was IL 9.6. Lowe's estimates of losses in the collectives
in 1954 ranged from IL 120 to IL 210 per family unit in the
various kibbutz groups. Converting the per capita security costs
to those per family unit would make it apparent that, at least
in the younger kibbutzim, security costs accounted for the bulk
of their losses in 1954. No data are given for subsequent years
but one can assume that the worsening security situation in 1955
and 1956 added to these costs. On the other hand, the much improved defense position of Israel since the Sinai campaign at the
end of 1956 must certainly have alleviated this economic burden
in most settlements.

The kibbutzim generally provide their children with a high
school education. The Ministry of Education pays teachers'
salaries on a per child basis, but as most of the classes are small,
the kibbutzim subsidize their children's education. The estimate
is that insofar as teachers' salaries alone are concerned, even in a
kibbutz of 100 families (and most kibbutzim have fewer than
100 families), the government budget covers only 60 to 65 per
cent of the salaries. The governmental policy regarding school
buildings and equipment is similar, forcing the collectives to invest
in this area sums considerably beyond the governmental allocations.

In addition to the health insurance which the kibbutzim (and
most of Israel's population) have, through Kuppat Holim of the
Histadrut, there are additional costs, not generally met with in
the city, which occur especially in those collectives located in
outlying areas of the country. All types of more specialized medical care which are provided in the large well-equipped urban
medical centers of Kuppat Holim involve not only the travel
expense to these centers, but what is even more important, the
loss of a day's work for every visit. This cost applies, of course,
to moshavim and other settlements situated in outlying areas,
which the kibbutzim pioneered in settling to a greater extent
than did other groups. Data for 1954 indicate that per capita
municipal expenditures in the moshavim were 39 per cent of
those in the kibbutzim.[24]

Psychological Factors. The Horowitz Committee Report points to certain indirect social and psychological differences between the kibbutz and moshav forms of settlement. In the former, there is a treasurer who is skilled in terms of familiarity with the financial institutions and whose full-time task it is to seek ways and means of enabling the kibbutz to carry out its various programs. In the moshav, the farmer is generally unfamiliar with these institutions and cannot easily take off time from his farm tasks for this purpose. The fact that the kibbutz is a much larger economy than the individual moshav farm makes lenders more willing to deal with the collective. The report further states that the moshav farmer is less prone to accept short-term loans, and is more likely to minimize current consumption in order to speed the repayment of his debts, than is a member of the kibbutz.[25] This type of analysis seems to confuse the symptom with the diagnosis. What the report may be alluding to, is the tenuous relationship between current consumption and current net income in the collective. What it does clarify is that, with respect to the older kibbutzim, the Jewish Agency had dealt less liberally with them than with the older moshavim. This is particularly true of the kibbutzim which were established between 1935 and 1948 (about one-half of all the collective settlements). The report estimates that in relation to the actual number of family units residing in the older kibbutzim, in 1956 the Jewish Agency had provided them with about 47 per cent of the approved settlement budget; in the moshavim, the estimate was 67 per cent.[26] A case study by Lowe of a neighboring kibbutz and moshav, both about 35 years old at the time of the study in 1957, comes to a similar conclusion. The kibbutz received a total of IL 15,000 at 2 per cent, to be repaid over 50 years; the moshav received IL 56,250 on similar terms from the Jewish Agency. The kibbutz had to rely on bank loans to a far greater extent than the moshav.[27] Obviously, the Jewish Agency was aware of the fact that the kibbutz is an open society, anxious to accept new adherents, while the moshav farmer does not "readily" accept a stranger as a partner in his farm.

On the other hand, with respect to the younger kibbutzim, it would seem that they are the recipients of *special* aid from the Jewish Agency. The number of "directed" moshavim is much smaller than the number of "directed" kibbutzim, even though the number of younger moshavim far exceeds the number of collective settlements founded since independence.

Expansionism. Another policy of the kibbutzim which has more recently been recognized as erroneous, is the policy of investment and "expansionism" without due regard having been paid to the net profit which would accrue as a result of such expansion. No doubt this was partly a result of government policy until the later 1950's to increase Israel's production — especially agricultural production. The policy of the Jewish Agency with regard to agricultural production was even more extreme than that of the government. However, the kibbutz movement itself has had a strongly expansionist tendency since its early history. The rapid increase in assets and production, and especially in agriculture, has always been a source of pride of the movement and is very evident in all its publications. But all these factors have frequently contributed to the financial plight of the collectives. The loans granted by the Jewish Agency to younger settlements are not repayable until the settlement is considered well established and even then the loan is payable at low interest rates over a long period of time. On the other hand, they were granted after lengthy delays causing the settlements to enter the money market for loans, to enable them to proceed with their investment plans; these were increasingly short-term loans at high interest rates. As a rule the Jewish Agency loan was initially designed to finance 75 per cent of the projected investment; the rest had to be financed by the settlement. The Development Budget of the government, which is the major source of long-term financing for those settlements not under the aegis of the Jewish Agency, frequently covered 60 per cent of the total cost of investment for which the loan was granted. These loans were for a much shorter duration than those of the Jewish Agency, with interest rates (between 1955 and 1958) ranging from 6.5 per cent to 8 per cent. Since even the older settlements had little, if any, savings, and frequent deficits, this induced them to seek inappropriate commercial loans. Loans granted for housing were for a period of fourteen years.

Loans for investment in fruit plantations were immediately payable, though the farmer must wait a number of years before deriving any income from the plantation. As a result, the financial structure was continually deteriorating. Thus between 1952 and 1958, total debts of the kibbutz settlements increased 5.3 times. Short-term debts (less than four years) increased 5.8 times, and long and intermediate-term debts (four years and over) in-

creased 4.9 times. Within the category of short-term debts, however, the accounts and notes payable showed the sharpest increase;
and while these carry no nominal interest rate, the hidden charges
far exceed even the high interest rates prevalent in Israel's commercial banks. Since 1954, loans both from the government and
to a lesser extent from the Jewish Agency have been "tied" either
to the official exchange rate of the Israeli pound in terms of
American dollars, or in relation to the cost of living index in
Israel. Thus the settlement would be required to pay, in addition
to the interest rate, the revaluated amount of the principal in
accordance with either the dollar-Israeli pound exchange rate or
the cost of living index.

In 1956 the government eased the financial plight of the settlements (mainly kibbutzim) by extending the period of repayment
from eleven to thirteen years, beginning with 1956. The Jewish
Agency, which has increased the number of "directed kibbutzim"
to approximately one hundred, provided funds for the repayment
of the short-term debts of these settlements. These so-called
conversion loans of the government, designed to ease the financial
plight of the settlements which had borrowed heavily in the short-
term money market to finance long-term investments, have been
instrumental in lowering the effective interest rate paid by the
kibbutzim since 1960. Annual interest payments as a percentage
of the total debts of the kibbutzim increased steadily throughout
the 1950's, from 2.5 per cent in 1950 to 6.3 in 1959. Thereafter
the effect of government aid, a lessening of the pace of investment, and an improvement in profitability began to induce a
decline to 6.0 per cent in 1960; 5.7 per cent in 1961; 5.3 per cent
in 1962; and 5.5 per cent in both 1963 and 1964.

The above percentages do not, however, reflect the full burden
of interest costs which was rapidly increasing throughout the
1950's. The total debts of the kibbutzim include an increasing
percentage of accounts and notes payable, which bear no nominal
interest cost but have considerable hidden costs. They also include
the Jewish Agency long-term loans, which the younger kibbutzim have yet to begin to repay and the older kibbutzim have often
been allowed to defer payment both of principal and interest.
If these categories of debts are deducted, the average interest rate
would be much higher than is indicated in the above figures.
Furthermore, the average for all the kibbutzim understates the
effective interest rate paid by the older kibbutzim (not receiving

aid from the Jewish Agency), which averaged 10 per cent in 1959.[28]

A better indication of the real burden of interest payments would be to relate them to gross and net production. Between 1956 and 1958, interest payments amounted to 8 per cent of gross production; in 1959 and 1960 they increased to 10 per cent of gross production; in 1961 the ratio declined to 9 per cent; to 8 per cent in 1962; and to 8.6 per cent in both 1963 and 1964. In terms of net production the estimate would be approximately double that of gross production.

In the moshavim, the per family burden of interest costs are known to be much less. Dr. Yehuda Lowe, who made a case study of two old, very well-established neighboring settlements — a kibbutz and a moshav — found that in 1957, per family interest payments in the kibbutz were 138 per cent greater than in the moshav.[29] While one may not draw a general conclusion from this one case study, it would seem that these figures are indicative of certain orders of magnitude. The above case study further points out that in terms of fixed productive assets (evaluated in real terms) the moshav had approximately double that of the kibbutz, primarily because of the large investment in livestock; total assets per family unit were 70 per cent higher in the moshav.

Although the financial plight of the kibbutzim may have been caused partially by the erroneous policies of the government and the Jewish Agency, there is no doubt that the policy of expansionism in the kibbutzim is an equally important factor. The publications of the movement are replete with retrospective criticism of this policy. One writer [30] lists the following: (1) investment beyond the capacity of utilization; (2) additional mechanization to cover up for inefficiencies in certain sectors of the kibbutz economy; (3) investment for the sake of expansion, even though the branch to be expanded is not well organized; (4) unnecessary additional buildings without full utilization of existing facilities; (5) expensive buildings where future adaptations were not properly considered; (6) allocation of investment funds between consumption and production was weighted in favor of the former; (7) building of expensive homes for the members, children's homes, and communal buildings, beyond the financial ability of the settlement; (8) insufficient development of industrial enterprises; and (9) lack of utilization of employment opportunities in industrial enterprises in which the kibbutz is a partner.

Surpluses and Subsidies. Since the appearance of agricultural surpluses in Israel in the mid-1950's, the agricultural parity index has become unfavorable for farmers. The exception to this rule is citriculture in which the bulk of the crop is for export at international prices. The kibbutzim, which only very recently have begun to expand their citrus plantations on a larger scale, were adversely affected by the "farm-price squeeze." The Horowitz Committee reported that between 1954 and 1958 prices received by non-citrus farmers increased 24.5 per cent, while prices of agricultural inputs increased by 32.0 per cent.[31] In 1959, agricultural production (in physical quantities) increased 17 per cent causing a decline of 10 per cent in the prices received by farmers. In the non-citrus sectors, the price declines averaged 20 per cent; in dairy and poultry, 37 per cent;[32] the latter affected the moshav sector more than the kibbutz sector. It might also be mentioned that the consumer price index rose 1.8 per cent during that year. Between 1959 and 1962 the parity index continued to be unfavorable. Thus between 1959 and 1962 prices of outputs in non-citrus agriculture increased by 13 per cent, and those of agricultural inputs, by 24 per cent.[33] The sharp price decline in non-citrus fruits in 1959 affected the collectives more than the other agricultural sectors since they produce the bulk of these fruits.

The large surpluses of agricultural products after the mid-1950's have increasingly brought about governmental intervention in the form of production controls and subsidies. These subsidies take many forms. They involve subsidization of the cost of irrigation water, fertilizers, and other inputs, and they involve direct subsidies for production. The granting of "directed credit" for certain areas of production is, under the conditions prevailing in Israel, a kind of subsidy in the form of lower interest costs than would obtain in the private money market. The manipulation of foreign exchange rates constitutes another form of indirect subsidization.

Tables 17 and 18 give an indication of the branches of agriculture which have benefited most from governmental and Jewish Agency subsidies.

Table 17 does *not* constitute the total subsidization of agriculture in these years. There were additional subsidies to the younger settlements, and low exchange rates for the importation of animal fodder. According to Raanan Weitz,[34] Director of the Settlement Department of the Jewish Agency, the inclusion of these indirect subsidies would raise total subsidies to agriculture in both 1955 and 1956 to IL 23 million, instead of the IL 13.3 million for 1955 and IL 16.9 million in 1956 given in the Bank of Israel report. Moreover, even Weitz's calculations do not include drought compensation damages, subsidization of water, and other indirect grants. On the other hand, it should be emphasized that subsidies to agriculture until 1958 were partially designed to keep down the controlled prices of agricultural products to the consumer. With the abolition of most price controls since 1958, the prime purpose of subsidies is to raise agricultural incomes.

TABLE 17. SUBSIDIES TO AGRICULTURE, 1954–1958
(in millions of Israeli pounds)

PRODUCT	1954	1955	1956	1957	1958
Milk	3.5	4.3	7.6	9.0	11.7
Eggs	—	—	1.4	2.9	4.0
Vegetables	2.4	5.5	4.8	12.7	21.3
Other products	0.8	3.5	3.1	6.6	4.9
Total	6.7	13.3	16.9	31.2	41.9

Source: Bank of Israel, Annual Report, 1959 (Jerusalem, May 1960), p. 139.
Note: The above is a partial list of subsidies as compared with Table 18.

TABLE 18. SUBSIDIES TO AGRICULTURE, 1959–1964
(in millions of Israeli pounds)

PRODUCT	1959	1960	1961	1962	1963	1964
Milk	16.2	12.5	10.5	20.1	26.9	32.2
Meat	0.8	3.3	1.1	6.2	8.7	8.1
Eggs	11.9	19.4	19.2	17.9	20.2	27.0
Vegetables	7.7	5.1	3.2	4.8	14.6	11.0
Cotton	4.8	6.8	8.7	10.0	10.6	10.7
Other products	0.2	1.1	1.7	2.1	4.8	8.7
Special subsidies to new settlements	2.6	2.9	2.8	2.6	1.6	1.0
Drought compensation	6.2	23.2	4.5	8.0	12.7	2.5
Fertilizer and water	3.7	3.4	5.4	6.8	5.7	22.9
Total subsidies	54.1	77.7	57.1	78.5	106.7	124.1

Source: Bank of Israel, Annual Report, 1962, p. 172, and Annual Report, 1964, p. 249.

Table 18 gives a fuller picture of subsidization than that presented in Table 17. However, as the Bank of Israel Annual Report for 1961 points out,[35] these do not include the value of various tax concessions, discounts, the hidden subsidy involved in the purchase of domestic wheat and sugar beets at prices above the international level, and other forms of subsidization.

Obviously these payments raise the profitability of agriculture in general including that of the kibbutzim. The question to be examined is, does the kibbutz movement receive a share of these subsidies commensurate with its share of total agricultural production in Israel? A cursory inspection of the data will immediately reveal that the bulk of the subsidies are in the dairy, poultry, and vegetable branches. Clearly, the moshav sector which has increasingly specialized in these branches has been the major beneficiary of subsidization. Kaddar estimated that in 1957 the established moshavim derived 8 per cent of their gross income from subsidies as compared with 2.4 per cent in the established kibbutzim. In the newer moshavim, from 12 per cent to 21 per cent of their gross income was obtained through subsidies as compared with 5.7 per cent in the newer kibbutzim.[36] In terms of net income the percentage derived from subsidies was much higher. The increasing subsidization of dairy and poultry since 1958 and the decreasing share of the kibbutzim in these branches indicate a continuation of this trend. The proposal of Hakibbutz Hameuhad Federation that subsidies be granted to agriculture not on the basis of per unit production of certain products, but on the basis of an equal subsidy per family unit, is an implicit recognition of this disparity and an attempt to have it rectified.[37]

Political and Federation Activities. A self-imposed burden, which the kibbutzim bear, lies in the area of political and federation activities. To the extent that they do this as members of the Knesset (Parliament), paid officials of the government, Jewish Agency, the Histadrut, and their affiliated political parties, there is probably a net gain accruing to the kibbutz. The salaries of these officials often exceed the income which would be derived by their employment in the kibbutz economy. In addition there are the many indirect benefits gained by the collectives, which have been discussed earlier. But, to the extent that the kibbutzim are requested by their federations to provide money and unpaid officials for political activities, affiliated youth organizations, and activities of the federation itself, there is an *immediate* burden which the income-producing branches of the collective economy must bear. The direct cash expenditure is relatively minor. The main burden is in terms of labor-days. In the established kibbutzim, the number of unpaid labor-days devoted to these activities in 1955 averaged 12.3 per worker. In the settlements founded after 1935, the average was 8.3.[38] The labor force summaries of Hakibbutz Ha'artzi Federation indicate that between 1958 and 1964 the average number of labor-days for all their kibbutzim was between 11 and 12.5 per worker.[39] The norms set by the kibbutz movement as a whole for 1963 indicate an average of 10 labor-days per member in the youngest settlements, 12 labor-days in the "middle-aged" group (presumably, those founded between 1935 and 1947), and 15 labor-days in the oldest settlements (presumably those founded before 1935).[40] To put these figures in their proper perspective they should be compared to the number of labor-days devoted to the internal administration of the kibbutz. The data indicate that the burden of these unpaid activities was approximately equal to, and even exceeded, the number of labor-days devoted to internal administration. If these labor-days are converted to their monetary equivalent and added to the small per capita money expenditure which the kibbutzim devote to these activities, they would provide an explanation for a substantial portion of the deficits incurred by the collective settlements. In fact, following Lowe's calculation of kibbutz deficits, it would seem that the burden of these activities upon the older kibbutzim in 1955 would be wholly explained by the loss of this manpower to the income-producing branches. In the other groups of kibbutzim it would explain between one-third and one-half of their losses per family unit.

On the other hand, it is essential to distinguish between the immediate burden of these political and federation activities and their long-run benefits (economic as well as non-economic) to the kibbutz movement. A considerable part of these activities is in the form of direct aid to the younger settlements, many of which would not survive without the aid of the federations. The activities designed to recruit reinforcements to the kibbutz movement are crucial for the continued existence of many collectives. The various departments of the federations devoted to joint purchasing, guiding the settlements in their building plans, and organizing their consumption and production branches, have a direct beneficial economic effect upon the collectives (mostly the younger ones which are relatively inexperienced). On balance, the conclusion is that the older, better-established kibbutzim bear a considerable immediate direct burden which weakens the profitability of their economy, the younger settlements being the net beneficiaries. There is nothing analogous to this in the various moshav federations. Moshav farmers cannot be readily "released" from their farms to devote themselves to unpaid political or communal activities. Even the urban worker who might be inclined to devote some of his free evenings to unpaid political activity would not be in a position to take leave from his regular job for the sake of political or communal activities. The unique structure of the collectives enables such activities, but does not obviate the burden which they impose upon the settlement.

Population Shift. Since the mid-1950's there has been a continual shift of population from the rural-agricultural sectors to the cities and towns. This has been taking place in spite of an official policy which has been designed to restrain this trend. Thus, although the number of moshavim increased from 333 in 1956 to 345 in 1962, the total moshav population declined from 123.9 thousand to 119.1 thousand. The addition of many new moshavim and the high birthrate did not change this trend. In the 228 kibbutzim the population declined from 79.7 thousand in 1956 to 79.4 thousand in 1962. The moshav population declined by 3.9 per cent; the kibbutz population, 0.4 per cent. Considering the fact that the number of moshavim increased by 12, whereas the number of kibbutz settlements did not increase, it is evident that the population exodus from the moshav settlements existing in 1956 was far greater than that in the kibbutz sector. In fact there were 1,800 abandoned family farms in 1962 in the existing moshavim, and ten moshavim were completely abandoned.[41] Investigations have shown that even in the established moshavim, every third or fourth farm serves as a place of residence, with the "farmer" deriving most of his income from outside employment. Superficially, this too would seem to be analogous to the situation in the collectives. It was estimated that in 1959 the older kibbutzim had 14,000 family units out of the 16,000 family units for which they were planned. In the newer kibbutzim the situation was much worse; they numbered but 4,000 out of the 10,000 family units planned for them.[42]

A more recent report states that in terms of agricultural family units the older kibbutzim received allocations on the basis of 15,295 family units and actually had 11,296; the younger kibbutzim received allocations on the basis of 14,370 units and had 5,192 family units. Similarly, the older moshavim received allocations on the basis of 5,837 units and had 5,308; the newer moshavim received allocations on the basis of 20,243 units and actually had 16,517 family units engaged in agriculture.[43] Furthermore, the writer of this report feels that the "official" figures are considerably inflated in terms of the actual number of family units in the kibbutzim and moshavim. The similarity ends here, however. The effect of the population decline upon the kibbutzim is diametrically opposite to that upon the moshavim. The fact that the moshav farmer's neighbor is working in town instead of cultivating his farm is important in terms of its impact upon the national economy, insofar as it involves a wastage of national resources. It does not have any significant effect upon the farmer's private profitability. On the contrary, he might very well welcome the diminution of the number of rivals, especially since the appearance of agricultural surpluses in Israel. In the kibbutz, the structure of collective consumption and production involves a high degree of fixed costs in terms of money expenditures, personal services, and even more in terms of administrative overhead. Thus the average costs, in labor-days and money, of providing for a small population are higher in a small kibbutz. In the area of production, the economies of scale attainable in large branches are unattainable in the small kibbutz restricted by limited manpower available for the income-producing branches and the aversion to the use of hired labor. The administrative staff becomes disproportionately large in relation to the manpower available for income-producing work.

In the moshav, it will usually be the least successful farmers who leave; in the kibbutz there is no basis for such a presumption. One might even argue that frequently the more skilled and more capable kibbutz members are enticed by the employment opportunities available to them elsewhere. The so-called average moshav, even in the older moshavim, is in essence a residual, which would generally include the more successful farmers. This attrition is similar to that which prevails in any private enterprise economy, leaving, over a period of time, those better adapted to farming. In the collective, once it falls below a certain minimal number of family units, even the departure of unskilled and less capable members adds significantly to the burden of those remaining. There are various estimates offered for the minimal number of family units which a kibbutz requires to make it a viable community in the social as well as the economic sense. The major problem facing the younger kibbutzim is that so many of them have failed to reach this minimum by any standards.

The collective settlements, as has been pointed out repeatedly, are not isolated communities. On the contrary, they are very much part of the social, political, and economic life of the country. The rapidly rising consumption standards in Israel have had a strong effect upon the kibbutzim. The average annual increase in per capita consumption in Israel between 1955 and 1959 was 5.3 per cent (in real terms). Between 1959 and 1964 the average increase was 6.5 per cent.[44] Recalling the estimate made in the kibbutz journal that in 1958 the real consumption standards in the collective settlements were equivalent to the higher standards of the better-paid urban workers (other than in housing), one can well estimate the continued impact of Israel's rising living levels upon the profitability (i.e., saving) of the kibbutz economy. The attraction which the urban economy has for the generally poorer rural population impels the kibbutz movement to try to "keep up with the Joneses." Other things being equal, this makes it even more difficult for the collective to balance its budget.

SIGNS OF INCREASING PROFITABILITY

Apparently other things have not been equal, since the estimates are that in 1961 and 1962 the kibbutzim, as a whole, did succeed in balancing their budgets and even showed modest real savings. What factors have wrought this change after (at least) seven consecutive years of deficits?

Directed Kibbutzim. One factor has certainly been the Jewish Agency's system of "directed kibbutzim" which has been encompassing an increasing number of collectives. The Israel Government Yearbook lists 122 kibbutzim under the care of the Settlement Department in 1963 (including 12 that were founded before independence),[45] and according to an official of the department all of them will be "directed kibbutzim." [46] In these kibbutzim, the Jewish Agency repays the commercial loans which they had undertaken at high interest rates and which threatened them with insolvency. The loans of the Jewish Agency are not payable (principal and interest) until the settlement is considered well-established. Furthermore the Settlement Department plans the economy of these settlements in terms of labor force allocations, income and expenditures, and investments, and the various kibbutz federations provide the necessary managers for them. As a result, some of the economic burden which the older settlements had been bearing in support of the weaker members of their federations has been partially shifted to the Jewish Agency. According to the Audit Union, there were 491 members of the older settlements in the younger kibbutzim (October 1, 1962).[47] The fact that some of these have become salaried officials of the Jewish Agency has been advantageous for the economies of the older settlements.

Conversion Loans. Another factor is the effect of the various "conversion loans" of the public bodies (the government, Jewish Agency, and the Histadrut) which replaced a part of the short-term, high-interest commercial loans, with long-term low-interest loans. For the kibbutz movement as a whole this helped to reduce the interest payments as a percentage of total debts from 6.3 per cent in 1959 to 5.3 per cent in 1962. Excluding the kibbutzim founded since 1948, the decline is from 7.5 per cent in 1959 to 6.4 per cent in 1962. These loans saved the settlements approximately IL 3 million in interest costs in 1961 and a similar amount in 1962 (as compared with the rates they had been paying in 1959). For the kibbutzim as a whole, the combined effect of the "conversion loans" to the older kibbutzim and the "adoption" of an increasing number of younger settlements by the Jewish Agency (and the payment by the latter of the commercial loans of the new settlements) resulted in "saving" the kibbutz movement about IL 3.5 million in 1961 and double that amount in 1962 (calculated on the basis of the interest rates paid in 1959). Recalling the estimated surplus of IL 10 million in 1961 and IL 8 million in 1962, the role played by this form of public aid was substantial in 1961 and preponderant in 1962.

Apparently these steps have been insufficient for a number of settlements. A report published in July 1963 [48] stated that an additional sum of IL 30 million was being allocated by the above-mentioned public bodies to "consolidate" the debts of 30 settlements (mainly kibbutzim) founded shortly before Israel's independence, which were in the throes of a severe financial crisis. The report stated that the crisis was a result not only of their debt structure, which had brought about very high interest payments, but also of their internal management.

Improved Acreage Yields. Another factor of basic importance in explaining the improved economic situation in the kibbutzim in 1961 and 1962 is the considerable improvement in agricultural yields in these years and the relatively favorable price movements. The abundant rainfall in 1961 contrasted sharply with the drought in the previous three years, especially in 1960. The increase was reflected in the cereal crops — primarily grains — the output of which went up 80 per cent (in Israeli agriculture). Added to that was a slight increase in the prices of these products. Recalling the predominant position of the collectives in the production of these crops, especially the unirrigated ones, one can well realize its favorable effect upon their economies. Similarly the sugar beet crop (in Israel) increased by 41 per cent and enjoyed a price increase of 3 per cent as well. The cotton crop increased by 36 per cent, but suffered a very small price decline of 1 per cent. Another area where the kibbutzim specialize is in the non-citrus fruits. Partly due to the fact that many young vineyards and orchards reached the fruit-bearing stage in 1961, and partly as a result of the more favorable weather conditions, there were sharp increases in Israel's production of grapes (17 per cent), other deciduous fruit (27 per cent), and bananas (29 per cent). In spite of these sharp increases in supply, the price of grapes actually increased by 4 per cent, and that of bananas declined modestly (2 per cent) and of deciduous fruits more heavily (7 per cent). The Bank of Israel report explains that this was due partly to the increase in cold storage facilities, which enabled the regulation of supply, and partly to the increase in banana exports. Since the bulk of non-citrus fruits is produced by the collective settlements, these developments had a very favorable impact on their profitability. In the livestock branches, developments were also favorable to the farmers. The fact that the moshavim gained more as a result of their specialization in these branches does not minimize the gain to the economy of the collectives. Israel's production of eggs increased 16 per cent (as compared with the previous year) and poultry meat 20 per cent, while prices were constant. Production of milk increased but 2.3 per cent, but as a result of restricted importation of dairy products, prices rose 10 per cent. Production of beef declined 12 per cent resulting in a greater price increase (16 per cent) thus increasing the income from this branch.[49] All these developments in Israeli agriculture in 1961, had a very favorable effect on the economy of the kibbutzim.

The year 1962 was somewhat less favorable for Israeli agriculture than 1961. This was partly due to poorer weather conditions, which, however, were much more favorable than those prevailing in 1960. The decline in output of cereal crops was more than offset by higher prices. The data [50] for the kibbutzim belonging to the Ihud Federation show an increase in the production of cereals at a time when Israeli agriculture, as a whole, shows a decline of 11 per cent. Production of cotton in the Ihud kibbutzim increased 33 per cent in 1962 (as compared with 1961) at a time that, in Israeli agriculture, cotton production increased by 11 per cent. The price of cotton declined 3 per cent. Production of citrus fruits increased 40 per cent as compared with 6 per cent in Israeli agriculture, and prices increased 22 per cent. Prices of non-citrus fruits were unfavorable but production increases were generally greater. Poultry meat in the kibbutzim of the Ihud increased by 49 per cent as compared with 22 per cent in Israeli agriculture. The price decline of 3 per cent was relatively minor. Milk production increased by 18 per cent as compared with 12 per cent in Israeli agriculture, and prices increased 2.3 per cent. Beef production increased by 28 per cent in the Ihud kibbutzim, while in Israeli agriculture, as a whole, production remained constant. The price of beef increased by 3 per cent. The devaluation of the Israeli pound in February 1962 caused sharp increases in the prices of various inputs. The average increase was less than 10 per cent.[51] Apparently rising productivity, coupled with rising prices of agricultural produce, more than offset the increase in the prices of inputs. One cannot be certain that the data for the Ihud are fully representative of the kibbutz movement as a whole, but it would seem that a sample encompassing 32 per cent of the kibbutzim would generally reflect the developments in all the collectives.

Estimates for 1963 would seem to indicate that the kibbutzim as a whole succeeded in balancing their budgets, and in 1964 showed a net profit (saving) of IL 6 to 10 million. The oldest group of collectives (33 settlements) succeeded in showing a profit in 1963 and an even higher net surplus in 1964. The four other groupings show either a precarious balancing of their budgets in 1963 or net deficits. In 1964 the two groupings of younger collectives (136 settlements) continued to show deficits.

Hakibbutz Hameuhad Federation in an article [52] (published in 1965) analyzed the profitability of its 57 settlements in 1963. Eleven settlements are rated satisfactory. Another 12 are rated "unsatisfactory" due to a number of factors including unsuitable financing of investment, high interest costs and consumption expenditures above the budgetary allocations and beyond the ability of the economy to sustain. Their financial situation is described as "grave." These are being returned to the aegis of the Jewish Agency, which will provide the necessary financing and direction to cure their financial ills. Another four settlements (founded shortly before 1948) are described as having shown improved profitability and are therefore candidates for receipt of their final budgetary allocation from the Jewish Agency. Another five settlements were returned to the auspices of the agency a few years earlier. Twenty-five younger settlements (most of which were founded shortly after Israeli independence) are still under the care of the agency. This analysis of Hakibbutz Hameuhad Federation would seem to confirm the above estimates of the profitability of all the collectives.

Generally speaking, weather conditions were unfavorable to field crops and non-citrus fruits in 1963, major branches of collective agriculture. Partially offsetting these developments was the sharp rise in production and prices in cattle farming, and the continued increase in non-agricultural income. The year 1964 was most favorable to kibbutz agriculture. Weather conditions were ideal, bringing about a very sharp increase of 150 per cent in grain output (with very little effect on prices); cotton production increased by 16 per cent and prices were slightly higher due to improved quality; the value of poultry production increased almost 10 per cent (in spite of a small decline in price); the value of cattle products increased by 11.4 per cent (including a price rise of 4 per cent), and the shift in dairy production from the moshavim to the kibbutzim, which became noticeable in 1963, continued in 1964; fish pond production increased by 6 per cent (and prices moved up 2 per cent); and finally non-citrus fruit output increased by a steep 38 per cent causing some sharp price declines, though their total value increased and government subsidies were tripled.[53] All of the above are branches of Israeli agriculture in which the collectives have a major or a preponderant share, and the impact of these developments on their profitability in 1964 was considerable.

Non-Agricultural Enterprises. Another major factor contributing to the improved profitability of the kibbutzim has been the increasing trend towards non-agricultural enterprises. Unfortunately, the data available for these activities are very skimpy. Provisional estimates for non-agricultural production in the kibbutzim indicate an increase in real terms of about one-fourth between 1960 and 1962, and a similar increase between 1962 and 1964.

At a symposium held in Jerusalem in August 1963, Professor Haim Barkai of the Department of Economics at the Hebrew University presented data indicating that in 1959 the industrial enterprises in the kibbutzim (including the small workshops used mainly for local repairs) had equalled the *net* production of their agricultural branches.[54] Furthermore, net product per employed person was more than double that of the kibbutz agricultural labor force. Though these claims were disputed by members of the Faculty of Agriculture of the university, there is no doubt that a very marked shift has taken place in the economy of the collectives in favor of non-agricultural pursuits. Dr. Lowe (see p. 91) estimated that investment per worker in kibbutz industry is approximately half of that in agriculture. Furthermore, the rapidly rising incomes in Israel and the higher income elasticity of industrial products (as compared with agricultural products as a whole) would indicate a favorable market for these products. All this would probably be indicative of higher profitability and would also provide a partial explanation for the improved economic performance of the collective settlements in 1961 and 1962.

Increase of Membership. Finally, and very significantly, there has been a decline in the percentage of members leaving the kibbutzim, at least since 1959, concurrent with an increasing number of immigrants, especially from South America, joining them. Our previous discussion has made it quite clear that, other things being equal, an increasing membership in the collectives, especially in those which have less than 100 family units (and this applies to two-thirds of all the collectives), will tend to increase the profitability of the economy. Conversely, a declining membership will increase the probability of deficits (this is especially true when "key" members of the branches or highly skilled personnel leave). Between 1955 and 1959 the annual increase in the number of members, and candidates for membership, was between 1.5 per cent and 2 per cent. In 1959 there was a decline of over 1 per cent in the number of members and candidates according to the Audit Union reports. Considering the fact that members of affiliated youth organizations and others (a decreasing number) were joining the kibbutzim during this period, it would signify that a much larger percentage of members was leaving. This is borne out by data of Hakibbutz Ha'artzi Federation which indicate that the percentage of the membership leaving in 1955 was 3.4 per cent; 3.7 per cent in 1956; 6.1 per cent in 1957; 5.5 per cent in 1958; and 5.6 per cent in 1959.[55] Since Hakibbutz Ha'artzi Federation has shown the largest growth during this period among the three large federations (which constitute over 90 per cent of the kibbutz movement) one can assume that the percentage of members leaving their settlements was larger in the other federations. In fact between 1955 and 1961 Hakibbutz Hameuhad Federation showed a small absolute decline, indicating large defections from its ranks. Since 1959 there has been a larger increase in kibbutz members and especially since 1961. Hakibbutz Ha'artzi data show that the percentage of members leaving in 1960 was 4.9 per cent (as compared with 5.6 per cent in the previous year). The percentage leaving further declined in 1961 to 3.7 per cent and 3.1 per cent in 1962. At the same time there has been an additional source of recruits to the kibbutz movement, namely South American Jewish youth, primarily from Argentina. Undoubtedly the increasing anti-semitism there brought about an increase in Jewish emigration from that country to Israel, and the kibbutz movement has received a number of these immigrants. A recent report [56] stated that about 45 per cent of the immigrants from South America had joined kibbutzim. It estimates immigration from these countries in 1963 as approximately 6,000. Even if the percentage joining the collective settlements in the future is smaller than heretofore, it would add significant strength to the kibbutz movement.

The Central Bureau of Statistics has recently published data on population mobility in Israel.[57] In 1963 departures from the kibbutzim exceeded entrances by 2,883, and in 1964 the negative balance was 2,387. There is no indication as to how many of these were temporary residents, and the number who transferred from one kibbutz to another. Nonetheless, the above data would seem to suggest that the exodus of members from the kibbutzim, though it has diminished since the 1950's, continues to be significant. The kibbutz population increase in 1963 and in 1964 (about 1 per cent) is much less than the rate of natural increase.

VII

SUMMARY AND CONCLUSIONS

The first kibbutz was founded in 1909. It was formed, initially, as a temporary experiment, an alternative to the Zionist settlement policy of administering farms through an appointed manager, with hired Jewish labor. The success of the collective from the outset led to a more permanent arrangement. As time went on, the patterns of organization and of an ideology evolved, and by the latter part of the 1920's the basic structure of the modern Israeli collective had crystallized. Various kibbutz federations were organized, each differing from the other in political affiliations and religious practices, but with similar socio-economic bases. In addition to the established settlements, there were many kibbutz preparatory groups in the country itself as well as abroad, awaiting the first opportunity to fulfill their aspirations. The removal of immigration and land restrictions by the new government in 1948 brought a wave of collective settlement in 1948 and 1949. Kibbutz members (as well as many who had already left their kibbutz but retained strong ties with the movement) were among the political and military leaders of the State, and their influence permeated the fabric of the whole Jewish community.

However, the mass immigration following Israel's independence did not turn to the collectives. The individuals who were persuaded to pursue agricultural careers generally preferred the moshav cooperative to the collective form of living. By the early 1950's, the number of moshavim and their population had exceeded that of the kibbutz movement. By 1962 the moshav movement was, both in terms of settlements and population, over 50 per cent larger than the kibbutz movement. Defections from the ranks of the kibbutzim were very large in the first years after independence. The youth movements affiliated with the various kibbutz organizations, both in Israel and abroad, provided a much smaller number of new recruits.

Generally speaking, the 95 kibbutzim founded since independence, as well as some of those settled shortly before, constitute the "weak link" of the movement. These have been the recipients of considerable aid from the kibbutz federations, from the Jewish Agency, and the other public bodies, but their position, according to the Audit Union survey (as of October 1963) continues to be very weak. Both social and economic factors require a minimum number of members to enable the collective to be a viable community. The Jewish Agency's Settlement Department has generally considered 80 to 100 family units as the required minimum. Some observers pointing to the various temporary groups found in most collectives (Youth Aliyah, Nahal, and others) argue that 60 family units would constitute a viable minimum. Accepting even the latter estimate, an Audit Union survey indicated that over one-third of the kibbutzim had not reached this minimal number in October 1963. Most of these settlements had been in existence ten to twenty years.

The organizational structure of the settlement represents the extreme form of collectivism, both in production and consumption. There is a communal kitchen and dining hall, communal child care, laundry and other services in connection with clothing, etc. The economy is divided into semi-autonomous branches such as dairy, poultry, field crops, fruit plantations, vegetables, carpentry, machine shop, and others (depending on the regional variations in climate, rainfall, and so on). The consumption branches are similarly subdivided.

The veteran membership is usually skilled and almost always employed in the branch of its choice. The newer members (usually unskilled), the temporary groups, and the older children of the members constitute the floating labor force, and are assigned by the labor manager to work in the various branches, on a day-to-day basis, as he sees fit. Legally, however, even the veteran skilled members are subject to assignment to any branch, when seasonal labor fluctuations so require.

Though the legally supreme body is the General Assembly of the membership, actual management is in the hands of the Secretariat, annually elected by the Assembly. Each of the production and consumption branches of the settlement is headed by a member appointed by the Secretariat or General Assembly. In addition, there are many other committees annually elected by the General Assembly dealing with specific aspects of kibbutz life. Although elections are held annually, there is a limited amount of rotation of over-all management responsibilities. Of great importance to management are the detailed bookkeeping and accounting arrangements, which are subject to the guidelines and annual audit of the Audit Union of the Histadrut.

All but five settlements (out of 230) were affiliated with the various kibbutz federations in 1964. The latter have assumed an increasingly important role, and the very survival of many kibbutzim must be attributed to the strength of these organizations. They have, in effect, stabilized the organizational and ideological patterns. They have the power to assign manpower, buttressing faltering settlements. This power includes the "drafting" of members for organizational work in Israel and abroad and assignment to the weaker settlements, the placement of new recruits to the movement in certain constitutent settlements, the placement of youth groups and others of a temporary nature, and so on. More recently, the paucity of new recruits has induced them to assign the children of the older collectives to settlement in the weaker kibbutzim (after the completion of their national service in the armed forces). These federations maintain a host of organizations, including loan funds, joint purchasing, construction firms, shipping, industrial plants (owned directly by the federation), educational institutions and others. No less important than the direct aid of these federations to their constitutents is the indirect aid they provide through their influence upon the government, the Jewish Agency, the Histadrut, and other agencies. Though the influence of the kibbutz movement has waned since independence, it far transcends its relatively minor numerical strength. This has been of decisive importance to the economic development of the kibbutzim and frequently to their very survival.

The incentives which motivate the kibbutz member have at all times been a mixture of the economic and non-economic. Initially, the challenge of colonization and, later, the opportunity to escape from hostile European areas were the primary motives of most kibbutz members. However, the establishment of the State of Israel weakened the incentives of many of these members, as is evidenced by the high rate of defections at that time. Hakibbutz Ha'artzi Federation statistics show that 9.7 per cent of the members left the movement in 1949 and 9 per cent in 1950; this compares with the average 2–3 per cent annually before independence.[1] The economic security which the collective affords its members (so long as the individual elects to remain in the settlement) is now of greater importance.

The kibbutzim, as well as most agricultural settlements, receive land from the Jewish National Fund or the government. The bulk of their initial investment capital is provided by the Settlement Department of the Jewish Agency. The land is leased to the settlement on a long-term, renewable basis at nominal rentals. Until 1948, the collectives were generally restricted in their development by the limited availability of land for settlement. Since independence, they have more than doubled the holding of a kibbutz family unit.

What is more significant is the continual rise in the irrigated area. In 1947, 22 per cent of their cultivated area was irrigated. Although the large increase in the number of settlements and the expansion of landholdings in the older collectives lowered this considerably, by 1963 it had increased to one-third. The allocation of land differed during certain periods, and was subject to considerable regional variations as well. As investment proceeded at a rapid pace in new fruit plantations, fish ponds, and other branches, the overwhelming importance of field crops in the collectives tended to diminish. The rapid increase in livestock necessitated an increasing allocation of land to the production of animal fodder. The areas allotted to fruit plantations in 1963 was six and a half times that in 1947, with almost one-third of this area devoted to citriculture. Another important branch, one which the kibbutz almost monopolizes in Israel, is the fish ponds, which are found in the northern part of the country where water is relatively plentiful. The shortage of labor, which has afflicted most kibbutzim since the early 1950's, has induced them to reduce their vegetable branch. The inability to mechanize many operations worsens their competitive position vis-à-vis the moshav sector, although the introduction of greater mechanization of potato production has induced the collective settlements to assign almost two-thirds of the vegetable area to this crop in 1963.

The strong drive within the kibbutz movement towards expansion, especially in agriculture, has given them a near monopoly of certain agriculture branches in Israel and a dominant position in others. Though they provided 18.7 per cent of Israel's agricultural labor force in 1963, they cultivated one-third of Israel's cultivated area and a similar percentage of its irrigated area. Their share of Israel's fruit plantations has risen from 9 per cent in 1949 to 18 per cent in 1963, and they dominate the production of most non-citrus fruit. Though their contribution to Israel's very important citrus crop was but 10 per cent of the total in 1963, the increasing emphasis given to this branch in the collectives since the later 1950's should strengthen their position, and have a favorable impact on their profitability. The kibbutzim culti-vated 55 per cent of Israel's field crops in 1949. However, the greater growth of the moshav sector has reduced the collectives' share to about 40 per cent in 1963. The shift towards the moshav has been greatest in the production of vegetables. The kibbutzim cultivated 18 per cent of Israel's area of vegetable production in 1950, but only 12 per cent in 1963. The unusually large demand for eggs has stimulated a great expansion of production. About one-tenth of Israel's agricultural production consists of this product alone, the bulk of which is locally consumed. Due to the high yields of the kibbutzim and their predominant position in the production of (much higher-priced) eggs for hatcheries, the kibbutz share (in 1960) of Israel's production of eggs was 26.8 per cent and of poultry meat, 40.6 per cent. The dairy branch is another which was increasingly dominated by the moshavim. Here again, however, the higher yields in the collectives explain their higher percentage of Israel's milk production (31.5 per cent in 1963). Since the mid-1950's Israel has developed the more specialized raising of beef cattle. In 1963 the kibbutzim produced about 30 per cent of Israel's beef.

As a result of their heavy investment in agriculture and their increasing proficiency, the collectives have generally succeeded in keeping pace with, and exceeding, the very high growth rates of Israeli agriculture. In 1964 Israel's agricultural production had increased to a level of six times its 1949 level (in real terms); and kibbutz agriculture was seven times its 1949 level of production. The kibbutz share of total agricultural production in Israel has fluctuated between a low of 27.6 per cent in 1949 and a high of over 31 per cent reached in a number of years in the 1950's and between 1960 and 1964.

Non-agricultural enterprises assumed significant proportions in the collective economy during the period of the Second World War. During the period following Israel's independence, the pace of industrial development slackened, but with the appearance of food surpluses since the latter part of the 1950's and the relative decline in the profitability of agriculture, the kibbutzim put re-newed emphasis upon their non-agricultural enterprises.

Even a complete enumeration of the non-agricultural enter-prises in the kibbutzim would not fully reflect the increasing shift towards industry. Many enterprises are set up as separate firms, frequently located outside the collective settlement, though they are owned and managed by the collectives. Some are owned and operated by the kibbutz federations, and many others by regional councils dominated by the collective settlements. A recent article describing the activities of the "Shaar Hanegev" regional council (almost all kibbutzim members) which was organized in 1950 mentions the following: drainage, sanitation, and fire department; a regional school; a slaughterhouse for poultry; refrigeration plant; cotton mill; cotton-picking machinery; sugar beet pickers; garage for repairs of large machinery; tractor and fuel stations; sorting and packing of potatoes, and others. Each of these enter-prises is set up as a separate company, and employed about 500 workers in 1963.[2] Though most of the above occupations are related to agriculture, regional councils in the central and north-ern parts of Israel operate enterprises which are quite removed from the usual activities of farmers.

All the available data seem to indicate that the average annual increase in productivity in the collective agricultural economy has been unusually high, exceeding the very high rates prevalent in Israeli agriculture as a whole. Between 1949–1960, productivity in kibbutz agriculture increased at an average annual rate of 10 per cent. There is every sign that this rate of growth in produc-tivity has been maintained or exceeded, on the average, between 1959 and 1964. The gap in terms of production per agricultural worker between the kibbutz and the private (mainly moshav) sector may have narrowed, however, as the large number of new moshavim which were settled in the period following independ-ence have intensified their agriculture and accumulated agricul-tural and technical skills. Unfortunately, data are not available which would permit the calculation of productivity in the sepa-rate branches of kibbutz agriculture, though data on output per agricultural worker and agricultural yields generally indicate a higher measure of efficiency and productivity in the collective sector.

In 1963 the average yield per cow was 22 per cent higher in the kibbutz than that prevailing in the other Jewish agricultural sectors. (The average yield per cow in Israel is apparently the highest in the world, exceeding that in Holland by 2 per cent.) [3] The high yields coupled with the installation of milking machines and other labor-saving devices have been responsible for an annual average rate of growth in milk production per labor-day of 13.2 per cent, between 1949 and 1960. In the poultry branch, the gap between the kibbutz and moshav in terms of yields has been narrowing, though in 1959 yields per laying hen were 25 per cent higher in the kibbutz sector than in the rest of Jewish Israeli agriculture (mainly the moshavim). Various studies of the field crops, fruit plantations, the potato crop, and the more recently developed industrial crops indicate generally higher yields and smaller labor inputs in the collective sector and a rapid growth in labor productivity.

The complex structure and consequent lack of detailed data of the non-agricultural enterprises of the kibbutzim precludes a similar study of the productivity of these enterprises. One writer estimated that in 1959 production per worker in kibbutz industry and crafts was 16 per cent less than the average for the country. Excluding the small workshops (including only those working for the general market), he found that production per worker was approximately equal to that prevalent in Israeli industry and that investment in reproducible assets per worker was also similar to the Israeli norm. It is obvious that while the kibbutz enjoys a number of advantages in agricultural production as compared with the small-scale moshav farmer, both in terms of economies of scale and specialization, it enjoys no such advantages in industry. On the contrary, the severe limitations of capital and labor restrict the kibbutzim to such industrial enterprises which can be competitive on a small or medium scale. Further, the increasing liberalization of import restrictions is subjecting Israel's industry to the discipline of international competition. This contrasts with the more protectionist agricultural policies, including tariffs and other import restrictions, direct and indirect subsidization, large irrigation schemes, and many other forms of governmental aid, supplemented by the benevolent aid of the Jewish Agency and the Histadrut.

Our understanding of the economy of the kibbutz must necessarily be incomplete unless it encompasses the whole economy, namely the income-producing branches plus the consumption branches. The kibbutz has always strived to become a self-supporting economy as soon as possible after its initial act of settlement and to accumulate savings to facilitate the expansion of its productive capacity as well as the basic investments necessary in the consumption branches. A detailed analysis of the balance sheets and income statements of the kibbutzim point to a consecutive series of deficits during the period 1954 through 1960 and small surpluses in 1961, 1962, and 1964. What is more significant, the losses during this seven-year period were incurred by most kibbutzim, including many which were in existence over fifteen or twenty years. While most older kibbutzim were incurring frequent losses, most of the older moshavim were, in most of these years, accumulating profits. If the collectives had been less productive than the other sectors under similar circumstances, it might readily be concluded that low productivity and hence losses are inherent in a collective structure that lacks the incentives of a private enterprise system; however, productivity was generally higher in the collectives. Were the deficits endogenous in their nature? Our conclusions seem to indicate that some part of these losses might be attributed to the collective structure; another, to factors beyond the control of the kibbutzim. The factors listed here are not necessarily in the order of their relative importance.

External Factors Adversely Affecting Kibbutz Profitability

1. Most kibbutzim are in outlying parts of the country, which involves higher security and marketing costs, consumption expenditures, and in many cases, higher costs of water for irrigation. These higher costs are net of governmental subsidies which absorb part of these differential costs.

2. Until the mid-1950's the kibbutzim generally received less than the other forms of settlement (mainly moshavim) from the Jewish Agency in the settlement budget. This induced them to finance their investments by means of short-term, high-interest loans, which had a *cumulative* negative effect on their profitability. The actual grant of these loans was frequently delayed on account of the financial difficulties of the Jewish Agency, further aggravating the weak financial structure of the collectives.

3. The governmental Development Budget provided loans to the established settlements (those which were no longer entitled to the aid of the Jewish Agency) in order to stimulate the development of particular agricultural branches that were deemed desirable from the national point of view. However, these loans generally provided no more than 60 per cent of the necessary financing. If the kibbutzim had been able to finance the difference

from their savings, there would have been no adverse effect upon their economy, but the lack of savings compelled them to borrow the remainder from commercial banks in the form of short-term, high-interest loans. Furthermore, repayment of principal and interest of the Development Budget loans began immediately, before the new investments had been transformed into additional cash income.

4. The failure of the kibbutz movement to attract youth to their settlements after 1948 in any appreciable number thwarted the anticipated growth of about half of the kibbutz settlements (those settled shortly before independence and the large number settled in the first years following independence). Many of the older settlements suffered considerable defections without receiving the replacements that had been so easily obtainable prior to independence. The kibbutz federations, which are much concerned with the survival of so many newer and weaker settlements, "draft" many from the older settlements to provide direct and indirect aid to their weaker constituents. The growth of these federations and their manifold activities strain the already difficult manpower situation of the collectives and impose considerable costs not borne by either the private or cooperative sectors in Israel.

5. The adverse parity index of agricultural prices was more pronounced in those branches in which the kibbutzim specialized.

6. A large number of kibbutzim are in areas with inferior soil, inadequate rainfall, and periodic drought. Governmental drought subsidies minimize these losses but do not make them viable economies.

7. Larger subsidies and other forms of public aid were granted to the dairy, poultry, and vegetable branches — prime specialties of the moshavim.

8. The educational policy of the kibbutzim adds to the high per capita municipal costs borne by these settlements.

Internal Factors Adversely Affecting Kibbutz Profitability

1. A diversified economy, while minimizing income fluctuations and the seasonal fluctuations in labor force requirements, is generally less profitable than an economy specializing in one or a few large-scale branches. Certainly the extreme to which most younger kibbutzim carried this principle of diversification di-

minished their profitability for a long period of time. Fewer and larger branches would have meant a smaller per capita investment, greater economies of scale, a smaller overhead in the form of administrative personnel and better utilization of the more experienced labor force and management.

2. Opposition to the use of hired labor has restricted the development of the more profitable branches. Furthermore, this ideology has compelled the kibbutzim to become more capital intensive, further aggravating their poor financial structure and increasing their direct and indirect interest costs.

3. Of singular importance is the institutional setup of the consumption branches which necessitates a much higher number of labor-days than in the equivalent private family. The result is that the labor input of the moshav family in the family farm is estimated to be about 35 per cent higher than that of the kibbutz family. This has the effect of raising the labor costs of the income-producing branches in the kibbutz. No doubt there are improvements possible even within the existing collective framework, but it is doubtful if they can be of such magnitude as to obviate this disadvantage *in toto*.

4. The standard of living in the kibbutzim has been largely divorced from their current profitability, at least since the 1950's. The standards are more determined by norms decided upon by the kibbutz federations. These norms are strongly influenced by the necessity to maintain standards akin to those prevalent elsewhere in Israel, lest the failure to do so cause increased dissatisfaction and defections. Though the federations pose these norms as maxima, they are considered by the membership and the managers of the consumption branches as minimal standards, with which the treasurer and the economic manager are "expected" to comply. Between 1955 and 1964, *real per capita* consumption levels in Israel have risen from 5 to 6.5 per cent annually. This steep rise in the general standard of living has exerted considerable pressure on the kibbutzim to follow suit. This, in turn, has had the effect of further raising the high labor costs of the income-producing branches and further worsening the profitability of the kibbutz economy. Furthermore, the ideological conviction that the kibbutz must afford its members the same degree of leisure (and even more) that exists in the urban sector reduces the number of man-hours available to the income-producing branches, further increasing the real labor costs of these branches.

5. The kibbutzim, because of their institutional setup, or their ideology, or both, did not shift their resources towards more profitable branches as rapidly as other economic sectors. Though the moshav was originally designed as a diversified farm, the moshav farmers, aware of the greater profitability of the livestock branches, rapidly shifted their resources towards the dairy and poultry branches or towards the very profitable citrus branch. The kibbutzim did this to a far lesser degree and at a slower pace.

6. The use of historical depreciation costs, as well as other misleading accounting procedures, has given the kibbutz managers and the members an erroneous concept of the real profitability of the economy. A more realistic understanding might well have reduced or eliminated some of their deficits.

7. Even within the existing institutional framework, it is widely recognized by the kibbutzim, as well as by disinterested observers, that varying degrees of waste and inefficiency exist which must be minimized.

8. The cost of political and other public activities imposed on the kibbutzim by their federations — mainly the drain on manpower — has further increased the burden on the income-producing branches by raising their real labor costs. In many cases, the number of men which the settlement has released for these activities equals or exceeds the considerable administrative overhead within the kibbutz. It is difficult to measure the extent to which these activities of the federations are of immediate, or long run, value to the constituent settlements. Certainly many younger, weaker settlements owe their very survival to their federations. More recently (1963) the kibbutz federations have joined in setting up a "Union" of kibbutzim, which would offer a united front in presenting their demands to the government, the Jewish Agency, the Histadrut, and other public bodies. (Each federation retains a veto power within this union.)

9. In a private enterprise system, the criterion of profit or loss will, sooner or later, tend to eliminate the unprofitable units. This raises the average profitability of the remaining units. In the kibbutz movement, the federations will rarely permit the dissolution of any of their constituent settlements. The effect of this policy is not merely to lower the "average profitability" of all the kibbutzim, but to lower the profitability of the stronger settlements as a result of the considerable aid they furnish their weaker counterparts.

10. While many moshav farmers have abandoned their farms (and in a few cases moshav settlements have been completely abandoned), there is a reasonable presumption that this was a decision of the less successful farmers. One can make no such presumption in the case of the kibbutz. On the contrary, it is frequently the enticing employment opportunities available to the more skilled kibbutz members in the cities and towns that has caused their defection, resulting in considerable damage to their collective. Furthermore, the institutional setup of the kibbutz is such that, even if a relatively unskilled member leaves, its economy suffers; this is especially true of those collectives with fewer than one hundred or even eighty family units. (As of October 1963, about one-third of the kibbutzim had 100 member families or more, and less than one-half of the collective settlements had 80 member families or more.) Consumption costs (especially in terms of labor-days) are higher in the small settlements, and the opposition to the use of hired labor minimizes the economies of scale attainable in the income-producing branches as well. Hakibbutz Ha'artzi Federation reports that the defection of members from its ranks averaged 5.6 per cent annually between 1949 and 1959.[4] Since this federation has emerged as the strongest during this period, one may presume that the defections were probably greater in many other kibbutzim, especially in the smaller settlements. The adverse effect upon the profitability of their economies, as well as on their social fabric, was certainly considerable. Before Israeli independence, the estimate is that from 2 to 2.5 per cent of the members left their kibbutzim annually,[5] but the great influx of new recruits during that period more than compensated for any loss in membership. The sharp increase in the number leaving their collectives after independence, coupled with a sharp decline in the number of new candidates for membership, must certainly be considered one of the prime causes of the poor profitability of the kibbutzim during this period.

REASONS FOR RECENT SURPLUSES

Thus far, factors accounting for (at least) seven consecutive years of deficits in the kibbutzim have been discussed. It is of equal importance to examine the reasons for the surpluses enjoyed by the collectives in 1961, to a lesser extent in 1962, the balanced budget in 1963, and the surplus in 1964. The following would seem to be most significant.

1. The system of "directed kibbutzim" had (in 1963) enveloped 122 collectives (out of 228). This means that the Jewish Agency has undertaken to plan, direct, and underwrite these settlements' economic activities and has forestalled the financial collapse which was threatening so many of them.

2. The above action has indirectly helped the older kibbutzim, as well, by partially relieving them of an economic burden.

3. Even the older settlements have been the recipients of large "conversion loans" (long-term, low-interest loans given by the government and the Jewish Agency) which have materially reduced the heavy burden of interest costs (direct and indirect) borne by these settlements.

4. The year 1961 and, to a lesser extent, 1962 benefited by favorable weather conditions; 1964's weather was especially favorable to those branches in which kibbutz agriculture specializes.

5. Price movements in agricultural produce were generally favorable in the specialty branches of the kibbutzim.

6. The fruition of large investments made in previous years, notably the fruit plantations and livestock, brought about large increases in production.

7. The parity index was only slightly adverse for agriculture, and this was readily offset by the continued rise in productivity.

8. The drive towards expansion of the agricultural sector has diminished considerably, and total (gross) investment in fixed assets even shows a decline in 1962 (in real terms).

9. The development of non-agricultural enterprises has, according to all reports, been generally profitable for the collectives, though precise data on the profits of these enterprises are unavailable.

10. The kibbutzim have become much more "profit conscious." This has expressed itself in many ways. The extremes to which they had carried out the "principle" of a diversified economy have been modified. There is a definite trend towards fewer branches and fewer crops, but on a larger scale. The settlements have utilized the expertise of trained economists to evaluate the profitability of individual branches, and in many cases are making use of input-output analysis to determine the most profitable utilization of resources. In these efforts they are being aided by agricultural economists in the Ministry of Agriculture and at the Hebrew University. Much greater emphasis is placed on the thorough training of the over-all economic managers in the

settlements in addition to the training of the managers of the individual branches.

11. Finally, and possibly most significantly, the collectives benefited from a larger increase in new members between 1961 and 1964, coupled with a diminution in the rate of defections of their existing membership.

In spite of the apparent improvement in the profitability of the collectives between 1961 and 1965, the financial position of many remains precarious. In July 1965 the Jewish Agency announced a special allocation of IL 45 million to 45 *older* settlements (including eight moshavim and two collective moshavim).[6] They are to receive 30-year loans at 3.5 per cent. Under Israeli conditions this amounts to heavy subsidization. Ordinarily, the government's bank of agriculture extends loans of much shorter duration at 10 or 11 per cent, and under Israeli credit conditions the latter are considered favorable terms. The government's Industrial Development Bank extends loans to favored industrial concerns at 11.5 per cent to 12 per cent. Furthermore, in August 1965 the Ministry of Agriculture announced [7] that IL 90 million will be granted in long-term, low-interest loans to the older agricultural settlements suffering severe financial stringency. The Ministry estimates that the gap between gross investment in fixed assets in farming, and the proper financing thereof, as IL 185 million, two-thirds of which applies to the kibbutzim. The reasons cited by the Ministry of Agriculture for the "gap" in financing have already been discussed in Chapter VI.

Conclusions

It has been said that revolutionary movements tend to become conservative with age. The kibbutz movement, which had played an increasingly important role prior to Israeli independence, looks with foreboding upon its declining position in Israel. The older collectives pin their hopes on the younger generation, born and brought up in the kibbutz. However, the younger generation sees the kibbutz as a natural type of social order; in fact, a young member will usually refer to his kibbutz as a "meshek" (an economy). If he decides to leave his meshek to live in a city or town, he considers this to be no different from a decision to choose one occupation rather than another, or to choose one place of residence in preference to another. He does not consider this (as do his parents) the forsaking of an ideal.[8] Many of the younger generation have left their kibbutzim after returning from service in the armed forces rather than elect membership in the kibbutz; in others, a large majority have chosen to remain as members in the kibbutz of their parents. In some cases, they have joined younger, struggling kibbutzim which, they felt, offered a greater challenge.

In a developing society, there is an increasing need for skilled professional people. This need runs counter to the "ideology" of the kibbutz movement and its affiliated youth organizations which stress the superiority of manual labor, rural life, and, particularly, agricultural labor. A recent article in one of the kibbutz journals [9] quotes a professor at the Hebrew University who criticized the kibbutz movement for its "conservative" views. The view of the professor was that the pressing need for Israel *today* is to increase the number of teachers and scientists, and that the kibbutzim and their affiliated youth movements continue to stress the need for agricultural laborers. He felt that many talented youths were wasting their potential in the performance of relatively unskilled work in the collectives.

Israeli youth is increasingly turning towards the professions. The more idealistic among them consider that work with the underprivileged and with the new immigrants from Middle Eastern countries, and establishment of urban centers in the Negev as no less a challenge than pioneering in a new kibbutz. This is the view held by the leadership of the country today, to the dismay of the kibbutz movement.

Another problem facing the kibbutzim is their adaptation to a growing industrial sector within the collective economy. To become competitive with the growing industrial firms in Israel and, to an increasing extent, to meet the challenge of international competition, there is a compelling need to develop large-scale industries. This has resulted in the development of industrial enterprises where the kibbutzim perform the managerial functions and derive the profits, but with a labor force consisting largely of new immigrants from North Africa and the Middle East. Although the working conditions and the wages meet the stiff requirements of the Histadrut, the personal relationship between the kibbutz members and their employees is often anything but harmonious.

Economic forces dictate an expansion of the industrial sector, and thus far they seem to have prevailed. At the same time, the resolutions of the movement to rid themselves of hired workers undermine any feeling of job security which these workers might have. This aggravates the relationship between the employers and workers and causes further disillusionment within the kibbutz. In the opinion of one of the kibbutz leaders, the drive for expansion and increased profits and the priority given to the income-producing branches have succeeded in increasing the assets of the kibbutz, concurrent with a loss of those values which underlie the very foundation of the collective society. One of the more notable aspects of this problem is the fact that the kibbutzim are curtailing their use of hired laborers (as a result of the increasing ideological and social pressures) by transferring some of their economic activities to the regional councils.[10] It has been noted earlier that these councils have developed many industrial and other firms, in addition to their municipal functions. There is a similar trend to transfer economic activities to central purchasing organizations and to the kibbutz federations. These organizations rely largely or mostly on hired laborers but are usually managed and owned by the collectives. This *may* provide a partial solution to the ideological difficulties. Whether the social problems are solved thereby is certainly doubtful.

In an article published in 1965 in one of the kibbutz journals [11] one of the leading members of the movement discusses the problems of saving, investment, and consumption as they relate to the collectives. He notes that both the moshav and kibbutz began without any capital and were financed by the Jewish Agency and other public bodies. The moshav seems to succeed in accumulating capital sooner than the kibbutz. This, in turn, complicates the financial structure of the kibbutz, further raising its interest costs, and so on. As a result of these financial difficulties a number of "conversion" or "consolidation" loans have been executed in the last ten years (by the government, the Jewish Agency, and the Histadrut). Nevertheless there are still many kibbutzim which are in need of additional special aid. The most serious aspect of this is the fact that not a few of these have been in existence a number of decades. "We are approaching a situation in which many, if not most, kibbutzim will be under the administrative supervision of lenders. It seems to me, that not many years ago, such a development would have been viewed as antithetical to the essence of the collective economy, as a danger and an insult which should be avoided at all costs. Today it is not unusual to find members who consider it 'ideal' to be returned to the auspices of the Jewish Agency or to become a 'directed economy'." Directly related to this problem of saving, consumption, and investment is the fact that since the mid-1950's the standard of living in Israel has been rising at a remarkable 5–6 per cent annually, and the average annual increase during the first half of the 1960's has been over 6 per cent (in the U.S. the comparable figure in the post World War II period has been 2 per cent). The kibbutz member has frequent contact with people in the cities and towns and with those possessing similar skills or administrative positions. He cannot help but be impressed and influenced by their high and rising living standards. The fervent idealism of the movement until the 1950's was able to convince many that they must "sacrifice" higher living levels for other goals. The "normalcy" that has prevailed since then creates intense pressures within the kibbutzim to raise consumption levels rapidly. Generally speaking, within any population, the highest rate of saving (as a percentage of disposable personal income) is among the employers and self-employed, in contrast with employees. The kibbutz is, technically, within the former category. Yet, the kibbutzim have either a low rate of saving, no saving, or deficits.

Many foreign observers frequently question the future of the kibbutz. Intuitively, they tend to consider that their future will be similar to that of other "utopian societies" which arose in various parts of the world and then disappeared. In the foreseeable future it is most unlikely that this will happen to the Israeli collectives. They are very strongly entrenched in the economy and society of Israel, and are very effectively organized in their various federations and in the recent Union of Kibbutzim. The federations have tended to assume increasing control of their constituent settlements and to that extent tend to restrain evolutionary changes within them. Certain modifications have taken place in the internal structure of the settlements since Israeli independence. A number of collectives have arranged for the children to sleep in rooms adjacent to that of their parents (during the day they are taken care of in the children's home of the collective). Many have arranged for members to have some of their meals at home rather than in the common dining room. Many have adopted the principle of determining a fixed personal budget for clothing, vacations, and sundry expenditures, rather than following the original principle of "to each according to his needs." These phenomena as well as some others would tend to indicate a trend towards less collectivization and more individualism. And yet it seems doubtful that this trend can go much farther without endangering the very essence of the kibbutz, which is based on collective consumption as well as collective production. Basic modifications of the collective structure require not only the decision of a majority of the membership within an existing settlement, but, what is infinitely more difficult, the approval of the kibbutz federation to which it is affiliated. Furthermore, within an existing settlement many structural changes usually entail large initial expenditures.

The kibbutzim believe that their future existence depends mainly on their own children. They have, implicitly, abandoned the hope of receiving recruits on a large scale. It seems that in recent years the number of new adherents has not even matched the defections from their ranks and that the small increase in population and members has been mainly due to natural increase and the decision of most of their children (after returning from service in the armed forces) to opt for membership. The education of the children includes a strong emphasis on the virtues of the kibbutz way of life. While the collectives provide all their children with a secondary education (in Israel only eight years of schooling are compulsory), most of them are not prepared for the special government examinations at the completion of high school, which permit entrance to a university. The fear that after graduation from a university, the likelihood of returning to the kibbutz is much diminished seems to be the underlying reason for this decision.

It may very well be that in the future, as in the past, there will be *isolated* instances of communal settlements being set up in other countries, inspired by the example of the Israeli collective. But it is most doubtful this can be done on the scale prevalent in Israel (without government compulsion). The unique conditions which prevailed prior to Israeli independence are unlikely to be emulated elsewhere. However, model farms, incorporating *some* of the principles and techniques of the Israeli commune might have a beneficial effect on the social and economic development of the less developed countries.

Within Israel it is likely that even if the population of the collectives continues its slow rate of increase, its percentage of Israel's population will continue to decline. Barring any continual large-scale influx of new recruits (and none can be foreseen) a number of the smaller and weaker settlements will continue to lead a precarious existence. It is only the tenacity with which the federations hold on to these settlements which ensures their survival. From a national point of view it may very well be that, in certain instances, consolidation and merger might be the wiser choice. The older well-established settlements, and some of the newer ones, with their large-scale, well-developd agricultural and industrial economies, will probably continue to prosper. After having played a central role in the emergence of the State of Israel, the kibbutz movement will probably continue to play a significant, though diminished, role in Israel's future.

APPENDICES I – XI

APPENDICES 1–XI

APPENDIX I

KIBBUTZ SETTLEMENTS AND POPULATION

YEAR ENDING DEC. 31	TOTAL POPULATION OF ISRAEL	JEWISH POPULATION	No. OF KIBBUTZIM	KIBBUTZ POPULATION	% OF JEWISH POPULATION
1949	1,173,871	1,013,871	211	63,518	6.3
1950	1,370,094	1,202,993	214	66,708	5.5
1951	1,577,825	1,404,392	217	68,156	4.9
1952	1,629,519	1,450,217	217	69,089	4.8
1953	1,669,417	1,483,641	227	73,299	4.9
1954	1,717,814	1,526,009	223	76,115	5.0
1955	1,789,175	1,590,519	225	77,818	4.9
1956	1,872,390	1,667,455	228	79,688	4.8
1957	1,975,954	1,762,741	228	79,891	4.5
1958	2,031,672	1,810,148	228	78,634	4.3
1959	2,088,685	1,858,851	228	77,890	4.2
1960	2,150,358	1,911,189	229	77,955	4.1
1961 (May 22)	2,179,491	1,932,357	228	76,961	4.0
1962	2,331,801	2,068,882	228	79,254	3.8
1963	2,430,125	2,155,551	230	79,833	3.7
1964	2,525,562	2,239,177	230	80,749	3.6

Source: Annual *Statistical Abstracts of Israel*. Central Bureau of Statistics, Government of Israel (Jerusalem, 1949–1964).

Note: The above data exclude between 190 and 192 non-Jewish residents in the kibbutzim from 1961 to 1964.

APPENDIX II

KIBBUTZ FEDERATIONS, DECEMBER 31, 1964

KIBBUTZ FEDERATION	No. OF KIBBUTZIM	POPULATION	% OF KIBBUTZ MOVEMENT
Hakibbutz Ha'artzi	74	27,778	34.4
Ihud Hakibbutzim Vehakvutzot	76	24,560	30.4
Hakibbutz Hameuhad	58	22,297	27.6
Ha'oved Hatzioni	5	1,363	1.7
Unaffiliated	5	789	1.0
Hapoel Hamizrahi	10	3,407	4.2
Po'alei Agudat Israel	2	555	0.7
Total	228	80,749	100.0

Source: Statistical Abstract of Israel, 1965, p. 31.

Note: The above data exclude 190 non-Jewish residents in the kibbutzim.

APPENDIX III

TOTAL CULTIVATED AREA
(in thousands of dunams)

Year	Israel	Kibbutzim	Kibbutzim % of Total
1949	1,650	754	45.7
1950	2,480	1,033	41.7
1951	3,350	1,228	37.2
1952	3,475	1,370	39.3
1953	3,550	1,386	39.7
1954	3,560	1,347	37.8
1955	3,590	1,353	37.7
1956	3,685	1,376	37.3
1957	3,820	1,377	36.0
1958	3,940	1,392	35.3
1959	4,105	1,391	33.9

Source: Annual *Statistical Abstracts of Israel*; Annual *Statistical Manuals* of the Audit Union for Cooperative Agriculture (Tel Aviv, 1949–1963).

Note: Estimates for 1963 indicate that in Israel 3,970,000 dunams were cultivated, of which 1,361,000 were in the kibbutzim, *i.e.*, 34.3% of the total.

APPENDIX IV

IRRIGATED AREA
(in thousands of dunams)

Year	Israel	Kibbutzim	Kibbutzim % of Total *
1949	300	82	27.3
1950	350	101	28.9
1951	470	123	26.2
1952	340	130	24.1
1953	650	198	30.5
1954	760	212	27.9
1955	890	269	30.2
1956	965	295	30.6
1957	1,100	331	30.1
1958	1,185	391	33.0
1959	1,235	418	33.8
1960	1,305	427	32.7

Source: Annual *Statistical Abstracts of Israel*; Annual *Statistical Manuals* of the Audit Union.

Note: Estimates for 1963 indicate that the irrigated area in Israel was 1,470,000 dunams and in the kibbutzim, 480,000 dunams — 32.7% of the total.

	in the kibbutzim	in non-kibbutz agriculture
* Average annual rate of growth		
1949–1963	13.5%	11.4%
1949–1956	20.0%	17.4%
1956–1963	7.2%	5.7%
1960–1963	4.0%	4.1%

APPENDIX V

AREA OF FRUIT PLANTATIONS
(in thousands of dunams)

YEAR	ISRAEL	KIBBUTZIM	KIBBUTZIM % OF TOTAL *
1949	355	33	9.3
1950	377	47	12.5
1951	392	50	12.8
1952	410	56	13.7
1953	433	63	14.5
1954	475	69	14.5
1955	515	74	14.4
1956	536	84	15.7
1957	598	92	15.4
1958	645	101	15.7
1959	680	110	16.2

Source: Annual *Statistical Abstracts of Israel*; Annual *Statistical Manuals* of the Audit Union.

Note: Estimates for 1963 indicate that the area of fruit plantations in Israel reached 808,000 dunams of which 142,000 were in the kibbutzim — 17.6% of the total. However, of the 142,000 dunams, 25,000 were cultivated by the Jewish Agency.

* Average annual rate of growth	*in the kibbutzim*	*in non-kibbutz agriculture*
1949–1963	11.0%	6.0%
1949–1956	14.3%	5.0%
1956–1963	9.8%	6.6%

APPENDIX VI

FIELD CROPS
(in thousands of dunams)

YEAR	ISRAEL	KIBBUTZIM	KIBBUTZIM % OF TOTAL
1949	1,130	622	55.0
1950	1,856	917	49.4
1951	2,229	1,081	48.5
1952	2,426	1,190	49.1
1953	2,614	1,246	47.7
1954	2,546	1,218	47.9
1955	2,560	1,208	47.2
1956	2,670	1,233	46.2
1957	2,726	1,238	45.4
1958	2,790	1,282	45.9
1959	2,915	1,259	43.2

Source: Annual *Statistical Abstracts of Israel*; Annual *Statistical Manuals* of the Audit Union.

Note: Estimates for 1963 indicate that in Israel 2,636,000 dunams were cultivated in field crops, of which 1,507,000 were in the kibbutzim, *i.e.*, 40.1% of the total.

APPENDIX VII

AREA OF VEGETABLE PRODUCTION
(in dunams)

YEAR	ISRAEL	KIBBUTZIM	KIBBUTZIM % OF TOTAL
1950	130,765	23,410	17.9
1951	149,554	24,693	16.5
1952	188,499	31,851	16.9
1953	222,563	31,977	14.4
1954	228,363	34,969	15.3
1955	216,479	34,052	15.3
1956	223,599	38,081	17.0
1957	220,759	37,345	16.9
1958	223,920	30,908	13.8
1959	211,614	29,193	13.8

Source: Annual *Statistical Abstracts of Israel*; Annual *Statistical Manuals* of the Audit Union.

Note: Estimates for 1963 indicate that in Israel the area of vegetable production totalled 233,073 dunams, of which 27,514 were in the kibbutzim, *i.e.*, 11.8% of the total.

APPENDIX VIII

NUMBER OF DAIRY CATTLE

YEAR	ISRAEL (JEWISH SECTOR)	KIBBUTZIM	KIBBUTZIM % OF TOTAL *
1949	37,705	14,627	38.8
1950	47,325	19,885	42.0
1951	60,230	23,248	38.6
1952	64,220	24,542	38.2
1953	69,440	23,142	33.3
1954	74,005	23,975	32.4
1955	73,000	24,311	33.3
1956	76,800	24,444	31.8
1957	88,700	25,860	29.2
1958	113,400	27,557	24.3
1959	129,700	29,014	22.4

Source: Annual *Statistical Abstracts of Israel* and Annual *Statistical Manuals* of the Audit Union.

Note: Estimates for 1963 indicate that in Israel there were 125,760 dairy cattle, of which 35,778 were in the kibbutzim, *i.e.*, 28.4% of the total.

	in the kibbutzim	*in non-kibbutz agriculture*
* Average annual rate of growth		
1949–1963	6.6%	10.0%
1956–1963	5.6%	8.0%

APPENDIX IX

NUMBER OF LAYING HENS
(in thousands)

YEAR	ISRAEL (JEWISH SECTOR)	KIBBUTZIM	KIBBUTZ % OF TOTAL *
1949	2,598	302	11.6
1950	2,912	452	15.5
1951	2,643	552	20.9
1952	2,570	519	20.2
1953	2,800	628	22.4
1954	3,300	716	21.7
1955	3,100	709	22.9
1956	3,500	784	22.4
1957	4,000	763	19.1
1958	5,500	929	16.9
1959	6,500	1,043	16.0

Source: Annual *Statistical Abstracts of Israel*; Annual *Statistical Manuals* of Audit Union.

Note: Estimates for 1963 indicate that in Israel there were 6,800,000 laying hens, of which 877,000 were in the kibbutzim, *i.e.*, 14.4% of the total.

	in the kibbutzim	in non-kibbutz agriculture
* Average annual rate of growth		
1949–1963	8.2%	6.9%
1956–1963	3.2%	11.5%

APPENDIX X

VALUE OF AGRICULTURAL PRODUCTION
(in millions of Israeli pounds — 1949 prices)

YEAR	ISRAEL	KIBBUTZIM	KIBBUTZ % OF TOTAL *
1949	44.4	12.2	27.6
1950	58.2	16.1	27.7
1951	61.2	18.4	30.0
1952	75.2	23.5	31.3
1953	81.4	23.7	29.0
1954	97.7	28.4	29.0
1955	106.5	33.6	31.4
1956	126.7	39.6	31.1
1957	139.8	42.6	30.5
1958	162.6	48.9	30.0
1959	187.9	53 (est.)	28.2
1960	194.9	61 (est.)	31.3
1961	217.9	68 (est.)	31.2
1962	236.8	73 (est.)	30.8
1963	238.7	76 (est.)	31.8
1964	269.1	88 (est.)	32.7

Source: Annual *Statistical Abstracts of Israel*; Hakibbutz Hameuhad Federation, "Agricultural Production" (Tel Aviv), (June 1959), p. 4; Rivon Lekalkala (March 1963), p. 102.

	in the kibbutzim	in non-kibbutz agriculture
* Average annual rate of growth		
1945–1964	14.1%	12.2%
1949–1956	18.3%	15.4%
1956–1964	10.5%	8.5%

APPENDIX XI

INVESTMENT AND CONSUMER PRICE INDEX IN ISRAEL

Year	Investment Price Index	% Change from Previous Year	Consumer Price Index	% Change from Previous Year
1950	100		100	
1951	136	36.0	114	14.0
1952	243	78.7	180	57.9
1953	323	32.9	231	28.3
1954	376	16.4	259	12.1
1955	415	10.4	274	5.8
1956	464	11.8	292	6.6
1957	493	6.3	311	6.5
1958	500	1.4	321	3.2
1959	505	1.0	326	1.6
1960	525	4.0	333	2.1
1961	572	9.0	356	6.9
1962	686	20.0	392	10.0
1963	727	6.0	419	6.9
1964	752	3.5	441	5.2

Source: Bank of Israel *Annual Reports* for 1961–1964.

Note: The sharp rises in 1952 and 1962 were due to the devaluation of the Israeli pound.

BIBLIOGRAPHY

NOTES

GLOSSARY

BIBLIOGRAPHY

The purpose of this bibliography is to give additional information for publications referred to in the notes and to suggest titles for supplementary reading. (H) after the entry indicates that it is in Hebrew.

BOOKS

Agriculture and Settlement in Israel. Jerusalem: Government of Israel and the Jewish Agency, 1958. (H)

Avinery, I. *Cooperative Almanac of Israel.* Tel Aviv: Israel Press, 1963. (H)

Ben Yosef, Avraham C. *The Purest Democracy in the World.* New York, London: Herzl Press and Thomas Yoseleff, 1963.

Bloch, A. *Ma'archot Hakibbutz.* Tel Aviv: Sifrait Po'alim, 1952. (H)

Darin-Drabkin, Haim. *The Other Society: Kibbutz in the Test of Economy and Society.* Tel Aviv: Sifriat Po'alim, 1961. (H)

―――― *Patterns of Cooperative Agriculture in Israel.* Jerusalem: Government of Israel, Ministry of Foreign Affairs, 1962.

Gaathon, A. L. *Capital Stock: Employment and Output in Israel,* Jerusalem: Bank of Israel, 1961.

Gadon, S. *The Paths of the Kibbutz and the Kvutza.* Tel Aviv: Am Oved, 1958. (H)

Granott, Abraham. *Agrarian Reform and the Record of Israel.* London: Eyre and Spottiswoode, 1956.

Grunwald, Kurt and Joachim O. Ronall. *Industrialization in the Middle East.* New York: Council for Middle Eastern Press, 1960.

Hacohen, Eliezer. *The Economic Basis of the Kibbutz.* Tel Aviv: The Afro-Asian Institute for Labor Studies and Co-operation, 1962.

Halperin, H. *Changes in Israeli Agriculture.* Tel Aviv: Ayanot, 1960. (H)

―――― *Changing Patterns in Israel Agriculture.* London: Routledge and Kegan Paul, 1957.

Histadrut. *Forty Years of the Histadrut.* Tel Aviv: Mifaley Tarbut Vechinuch, 1960. (H)

―――― Institute for Economic and Social Research. *Labor Economy, 1959–1962.* Tel Aviv: 1963. (H)

Histadrut Yearbook. Tel Aviv: Mifaley Tarbut Vechinuch, 1962. (H)

Horowitz, David. *The Economy of Israel.* Tel Aviv: Massada, 1954. (H)

Hurewitz, J. C. *The Struggle For Palestine.* New York: W. W. Norton, 1950.

Infield, Henrik F. *Utopia and Experiment.* New York: Praeger, 1955.

Infield, Henrik F. and Joseph B. Maier. *Cooperative Group Living.* New York: Henry Koozis, 1950.

Jewish National Fund. *The First Decade*. Jerusalem: Jewish National Fund, 1959.

Lowe, Yehuda. *Agricultural Economics*. Tel Aviv: Am Oved, 1957. (H)

Manoah, J. *The Kvutza and its Image*. Tel Aviv: Am Oved, 1957. (H)

More, Y. *Agricultural Accounting*. Tel Aviv: Sifriat Hassadeh, 1959. (H)

Muenzer, G. *Jewish Labor Economy in Palestine*. London: Victor Gollancz, 1945.

Prause, Walter. *Cooperation in Israel and the World*. Jerusalem: Rubin Mass, 1960.

Rubner, Alex. *The Economy of Israel*. London: Frank Cass, 1960.

Samuel, L. E. *The Israel Yearbook, 1960*. Jerusalem: Israel Yearbook, Ltd. Published annually.

Schultz, Theodore W. *Economic Organization of Agriculture*. New York: Macmillan, 1953.

—— *Production and Welfare of Agriculture*. New York: Macmillan, 1949.

Shamir, Joseph. *The Agrarian Problem and Kibbutz Settlement*. Tel Aviv: Sifriat Po'alim, 1953. (H)

Shatil, I. *The Economy of the Communal Settlements in Israel: Principles and History*. Tel Aviv: Sifriat Po'alim, 1955. (H)

Spiro, Melford E. *Kibbutz Venture in Utopia*. Cambridge: Harvard University Press, 1956.

Stigler, George. *The Theory of Price*, rev. ed. New York: Macmillan, 1952.

Tauber, Esther. *Molding Society to Man*. New York: Bloch, 1955.

The Challenge of Development — A Symposium held in Jerusalem, June 26–27, 1956. Jerusalem: Eliezer Kaplan School of Economics and Social Sciences, Hebrew University, 1958. See especially, A. G. Black, "Reflections upon Israel's Recent Agricultural Development and its Relation to General Development," pp. 199–212.

The Kibbutz Movement, 2 vols. Tel Aviv: Hakibbutz Ha'artzi Federation, 1954. (H)

Villard, Henry H. *Economic Development*. New York: Rinehart, 1957.

Weingarten, Murray. *Life in a Kibbutz*. New York: Reconstructionist Press, 1955.

Weitz, Raanan. *Our Way in Agriculture and Settlement*. Tel Aviv: Am Oved, 1958. (H)

—— *Agriculture and Rural Development in Israel: Projection and Planning*. The National and University Institute of Agriculture, 1963.

Zweig, Ferdynand. *The Israeli Worker*. New York: Herzl Press and Sharon Books, 1959.

ARTICLES

Abromowitz, Z. "Advantages of Large Farms," *Lamerhav*, March 23, 1960.

Argov, A. "Greater Production and Productivity," *Bakibbutz*, February 25, 1959.

Ber, Baruch. "Kibbutz Losses," *Ha'aretz*, May 23, 1958.

Brum, A. "The Agricultural Production Surplus Crisis," *Mibifnim* (October 1960).

Efroymson, C. W. "Collective Agriculture in Israel," *Journal of Political Economy* (February 1950).

Elizur, Y. "Kibbutz Industry," reprinted from Maariv in *Panim el Panim*, July 1, 1960.

Etzioni, Amitai. "Agrarianism in Israel's Party System," *Canadian Journal of Economics and Political Science* (August 1957).

Fellows, Lawrence. "Spirit of Kibbutz Fading in Israel," *New York Times*, June 18, 1961.

Fenichel, Z. "The Achievement of Cooperative Agriculture," *Hameshek Hashitufi* (August 1960).

—— "Three Forms of Cooperative Agriculture — a Comparison between the Israeli Kibbutz with the Soviet Kolkhoz, the Chinese Commune and the Mexican Ejido," *Hameshek Hashitufi* (July 1960).

Fikman, Yosef. "Strength of the Agricultural Economy," *Al Hamishmar*, June 15, 1960.

Garbiah, Hillel. "*Positive* Agricultural Policy," *Al Hamishmar*, May 3, 1963.

Gelb, Saadiah. "The Kibbutz and the Development City," *The Jewish Frontier* (New York), April 1962.

Gilshon, A. "Agricultural Economic Development," *Rivon Lekalkala* (November 1957).

Goell, Yosef. "Kibbutz Industrial Output equals Farm Production," *Jerusalem Post*, August 16, 1963.

Hacohen, Eliezer. "Demographic Development of the Kibbutz," *Hedim* (August 1959).

Horowitz, David. Report of a statement by Horowitz, in *Business Diary*, November 11, 1959.

Kaddar, G. "The Problems of Financing Agriculture in Israel," *Israel Economic Forum* (July 1959).

Kottler, Yair. "Kibbutz Members on Paper," *Ha'aretz*, September 7, 1962.

Livneh, Zalman. "Pioneers to the University," *Hashavua Bakibbutz Ha'artzi*, December 21, 1962.

Minsky, Shlomo, "With the Completion of the Second Million Jews in Israel," *Hedim* (April 1963).

Nachshon, H. "The Cooperatives and Collectives in Israel," *Rivon Lekalkala* (March 1963).

Oded, Yitzchak. "Kibbutzim need more Capital," *Business Diary*, January 20, 1960.

Rand, A. "Kibbutz Living Standards," *Hedim* (April 1959).

Rivkin, Arnold. "Israel and the Afro-Asian World," *Foreign Affairs* (April 1959).

Rosen, Shlomo. "An Uncompleted Mission," *Al Hamishmar*, April 22, 1960.

—— "The Kibbutz Movement," *Hedim* (July 1958).

Sadan, E. "Inputs and Outputs in the Kibbutzim," *Rivon Lekalkala* (November 1962).

Segev, Emir and Nachum Zvi Pesach, "Regional Cooperation: Shaar Hanegev," (November 1964).

Shalem, Dan. "Stages in the Development of the Kibbutz Economy," *Hedim* (August 1963).

Shatil, I. "Economic Problems of the Kibbutz," *Hedim* (April 1960).

—— "Mathematical Formulas and Reality," *Rivon Lekalkala* (March 1963).

Singerman, N. "Kibbutz Economic Developments," Hakibbutz Hameuhad Federation, June 15, 1960.

Weitz, Raanan. "Balance Sheet of Agricultural Settlement in the First Decade of the State of Israel," *Davar*, April 23, 1958.

—— "Problems of Profitability in Agriculture," *Davar*, June 18, 1958.

—— "Unprofitable Criticism," *Davar*, April 22, 1960 and June 18, 1958.

Yakovi, Gad. "Pricing Policy in Agriculture," *Rivon Lekalkala* (July 1962).

Zinger, Zvi. "The Crisis of Achievement," *The Jewish Horizon* (New York), April 1963.

Zingerman, Moshe. "Agricultural Settlements and their Economy," *Lamerhav*, June 24, 1960.

—— "The Kibbutz in all its Activities and all its Branches," *Bakibbutz*, March 5, 1965.

Zur, Zev. "Kibbutz Finances," *Mibifnim* (June 1960).

—— "On the Economic Problems of the Settlements," *Mibifnim* (June 1960).

—— "Towards the Convention of Hakibbutz Hameuhad," *Lamerhav*, June 24, 1960.

PUBLIC DOCUMENTS

Government of Israel. Central Bureau of Statistics. *Statistical Abstracts of Israel*, published annually. Jerusalem, 1950–   . (English and Hebrew.)

—— Department of Agriculture. *The Position of Agriculture in Israel, January, 1960*. A report of a Government Commission, David Horowitz, Chairman. Jerusalem: Government Printing Office, 1960. (H)

—— *Israeli Agriculture*. Report by the Joint Planning Center and the Economic Advisory Staff of Israel, December, 1955. Jerusalem.

Israel Government Yearbook, 1962–1963. Central Office of Information. January, 1963. (English and Hebrew.)

REPORTS

Bank of Israel. *Annual Reports*. Jerusalem, 1955–1964. (English and Hebrew.)

Falk Project for Economic Research in Israel. *Reports*. Jerusalem, 1954–1963.

United Nations. *Economic Developments in the Middle East*. Supplement to World Survey, 1957. New York, 1958.

—— Food and Agriculture Organization Report. Report No. 161, September, 1953. New York, 1953.

—— Monograph on Community Settlements. A Report of the Survey Mission Community Organization and Development in Israel, 1954. New York, 1954.

MIMEOGRAPHED MATERIAL

Audit Union of the Agricultural Settlements. Population of Kibbutzim. Tel Aviv, 1963. (H)

—— Census of Production. Tel Aviv, 1964. (H)

—— Statistical Manuals. Issued annually. Tel Aviv: Audit Union for Cooperative Agriculture, 1955–1960. (H)

—— Yalkut. Tel Aviv: Audit Union for Cooperative Agriculture. (H)

—— Yediot. Tel Aviv: Audit Union for Cooperative Agriculture. (H)

Gil, Benjamin Z. "Settlement of New Immigrants in Israel, 1948–1953. "A joint report of the Falk Project for Economic Research in Israel and the Central Bureau of Statistics of the Israeli Government. Jerusalem, 1957. (H)

Government of Israel. Ministry of Agriculture. Report of the Minister of Agriculture. 1963 and 1965. (H)

Hakibbutz Ha'artzi Federation. "Summaries of the Labor Force of Hakibbutz Ha'artzi." Tel Aviv. March 1960 and February 1965. (H)

Hakibbutz Hameuhad Federation. "Agricultural Production." Tel Aviv. June 1959. (H)

—— "Summaries of the Labor Force of Hakibbutz Hameuhad." Tel Aviv. October 1959. (H)

Kaddar, Gershon. "The Profitability of Agriculture." Pamphlet issued by the Bank Leumi Le-Israel, Ltd. Tel Aviv. April 1958. (H)

Lowe, Yehuda. "Agricultural Credit in Israel's Collective Settlements." A report issued to the United States Operations Mission to Israel. Tel Aviv. February 1956.

—— "Kibbutz and Moshav in Israel." An Economic Appraisal issued to the Ministry of Agriculture. Tel Aviv. August 1958. (English and Hebrew.)

—— "The Problems of Kibbutz Profitability." A report to the Ministry of Agriculture. Tel Aviv, 1959. (H)

Reply to the Land Reform Questionnaire of the United Nations. Jerusalem: Economic Advisor, Ministry of Agriculture, June 18, 1953. Jerusalem, 1953.

Rosen, I. "Kibbutz Economy." Unpublished report of the Economic Research Staff of Hakibbutz Ha'artzi. Tel Aviv, 1959. (H)

Rosenfeld, Eva. "Institutional Change in Israeli Collectives," Unpublished Ph.D. dissertation, Columbia University, 1952.

Vallier, Ivan Archie. "Production Imperatives in Communal Systems: A Comparative Study with Special Reference to the Kibbutz Crisis." Unpublished Ph.D. dissertation, Harvard University, 1959.

PERIODICALS

Al Hamishmar. Hebrew daily. Tel Aviv.

Bakibbutz. Hebrew weekly publication of the Hakibbutz Hameuhad Federation. Tel Aviv.

Business Diary. Hebrew weekly. Haifa.

Bahistradrut. Hebrew monthly. Tel Aviv.

Davar. Hebrew daily. Tel Aviv.

Economic Quarterly (see *Rivon Lekalkala*).

Ha'aretz. Hebrew daily. Tel Aviv.

Hameshek Hashitufi. Hebrew monthly.

Hassadeh. Hebrew monthly published by the Agricultural Workers Association. Tel Aviv.

Hashavua Bakibbutz Ha'artzi. Hebrew weekly publication of the Hakibbutz Ha'artzi Federation.

Hedim. Hebrew quarterly publication of the Hakibbutz Ha'artzi Federation. Tel Aviv.

Igerret Hashavua Bakibbutz. Joint publication of the Kibbutz Movement. Tel Aviv. (H)

Igerret Lahaverim. Ihud Hakvutzot Vehakibbutzim weekly. (H)

Israel Digest. English bi-weekly published by the Jewish Agency. Jerusalem.

Israel Economic Forum. English monthly. Jerusalem.

Israel Economist. English monthly. Tel Aviv.

Jerusalem Post. English daily and weekly. Jerusalem.

Lamerhav. Hebrew daily. Tel Aviv.

Mibifnim. Hebrew quarterly published by the Hakibbutz Hameuhad Federation. Tel Aviv.

Panim el Panim. Hebrew weekly. Jerusalem and New York.

Rivon Lekalkala. Hebrew economic quarterly. Tel Aviv.

Shituf. Hebrew monthly. Tel Aviv.

NOTES

INTRODUCTION

1. Henrik F. Infield, *Utopia and Experiment* (New York, 1955), p. 2.
2. *Israel Digest*, December 12, 1958, p. 3, and February 5, 1960, p. 1.
3. Arnold Rivkin, "Israel and the Afro-Asian World," *Foreign Affairs*, April 1959, p. 490.
4. Avraham C. Ben Yosef, *The Purest Democracy in the World* (New York, London, 1963), p. 124.

CHAPTER I: ISRAELI AGRICULTURE

1. *Agriculture and Settlement in Israel*. Joint publication of the Government of Israel and the Jewish Agency (Jerusalem, 1958), p. 23.
2. Amitai Etzioni, "Agrarianism in Israel's Party System," *Canadian Journal of Economics and Political Science*, August 1957, p. 366.
3. United Nations, *Monograph on Community Settlements*. A Report of the Survey Mission Community Organization and Development in Israel, 1954 (New York, 1954), pp. 29–30.
4. Report of Minister of Agriculture (Jerusalem), February 1965, p. 25.
5. *Bakibbutz*, March 5, 1965, p. 5.
6. Bank of Israel, *Annual Reports*. (Issued annually by the Bank of Israel in Jerusalem.)
7. Bank of Israel, *Annual Report, 1964*, p. 91.
8. *Ibid., 1961*, p. 182.

CHAPTER II: HISTORICAL AND INSTITUTIONAL BACKGROUND
OF THE KIBBUTZIM

1. I. Shatil, *The Economy of the Communal Settlements in Israel: Principles and History* (Tel Aviv, 1955), p. 40.
2. *Igerret Hashavua Bakibbutz*, October 20, 1960, p. 8.
3. Shatil, *Economy*, p. 61.
4. *Ibid.*
5. J. C. Hurewitz, *The Struggle for Palestine* (New York, 1950), pp. 27–28.
6. Shatil, *Economy*, p. 370.
7. Y. Lowe, *Agricultural Economics* (Tel Aviv, 1957), p. 194.
8. Etzioni, "Agrarianism in Israel's Party System," p. 366.
9. Shatil, *Economy*, p. 270.
10. Benjamin Z. Gil, "Settlement of New Immigrants in Israel 1948–

1953." Joint publication of the Central Bureau of Statistics of the Government of Israel and the Falk Project for Economic Research in Israel (Jerusalem, 1957), p. 110.

11. *Lamerhav*, December 12, 1962, p. 6.

12. Lowe, *Agricultural Economics*, p. 201.

13. Shatil, *Economy*, p. 186.

14. C. W. Efroymson, "Collective Agriculture in Israel," *Journal of Political Economy*, February 1950, p. 32.

15. United Nations, *Monograph on Community Settlements*, p. 22.

16. I. Avinery, *Cooperative Almanac of Israel* (Tel Aviv, 1963), pp. 83–94.

CHAPTER III: OPERATION OF THE KIBBUTZ ECONOMY

1. George J. Stigler, *The Theory of Price*, rev. ed. (New York, 1952), pp. 148–149.

2. Shatil, *Economy*, p. 106.

3. *Ibid.*, p. 100.

4. Abraham Granott, *Agrarian Reform and the Record of Israel* (London, 1956), p. 28.

5. Alex Rubner, *The Economy of Israel* (London, 1960), p. 102.

6. Shatil, *Economy*, p. 379; Audit Union of the Agricultural Settlements, *Annual Statistical Manual of Kibbutzim*, 1960, p. 7. These manuals of the Audit Union will be referred to hereafter as *Statistical Manuals*.

7. Rubner, *Economy of Israel*, p. 112.

8. *Statistical Manuals*.

9. *Ibid.*

10. Lowe, *Agricultural Economics*, p. 232.

11. Shatil, *Economy*, p. 169.

12. Lowe, *Agricultural Economics*, p. 232.

13. *Ibid.*, p. 203.

14. Government of Israel, *The Position of Agriculture in Israel, January, 1960* (Jerusalem, 1960). This report is known as the Horowitz Committee Report, after its chairman, David Horowitz, governor of the Bank of Israel, and will be referred to hereafter as the *Horowitz Committee Report*.

15. Shatil, *Economy*, p. 147.

16. Haim Darin-Drabkin, *The Other Society: Kibbutz in the Test of Economy and Society* (Tel Aviv, 1961), p. 156.

17. Shlomo Rosen, "An Uncompleted Mission," *Al Hamishmar*, April 22, 1960, p. 2.

18. *Panim el Panim*, July 1, 1960, p. 14.

19. Y. More, *Agricultural Accounting* (Tel Aviv, 1959), pp. 13–14.

20. Audit Union, *Yediot*, December 1953, p. 22, and October 1954, p. 23.

21. Shatil, *Economy*, pp. 122, 378.

22. Audit Union, *Yalkut*, December 1957, p. 11.

23. *Histadrut Yearbook* (Tel Aviv, 1962), pp. 389, 393.

24. *Bakibbutz*, January 27, 1963, p. 12.
25. *Al Hamishmar*, April 22, 1960, p. 2.
26. *Ibid.*, June 25, 1958, p. 2.
27. *Ibid.*, April 22, 1960, p. 2.
28. *Davar*, January 18, 1963, p. 9.
29. *Bakibbutz*, November 27, 1962, pp. 4–5.

CHAPTER IV: THE CHANGING POSITION OF THE KIBBUTZIM
IN THE NATIONAL ECONOMY

1. *Horowitz Committee Report*, pp. 49, 53.
2. Audit Union, *Yediot*, June 1959, p. 25.
3. Bank of Israel, *Annual Report, 1962*, p. 155.
4. *Horowitz Committee Report*, p. 47.
5. A. Bloch, *Ma'archot Hakibbutz* (Tel Aviv, 1952), p. 216.
6. Shatil, *Economy*, p. 242; H. Halperin, *Changes in Israeli Agriculture* (Tel Aviv, 1960), p. 162.
7. Gil, "Settlement of New Immigrants in Israel 1948–1953," p. 156.
8. Eliezer Hacohen, "Demographic Development of the Kibbutz," *Hedim*, August 1959, p. 25.
9. Shatil, *Economy*, pp. 242, 294; Halperin, *Changes*, p. 163.
10. Ferdynand Zweig, *The Israeli Worker* (New York, 1959), pp. 224–225.
11. Darin-Drabkin, *The Other Society*, pp. 279–280.
12. *Bakibbutz*, May 8, 1963, p. 2.
13. Bank of Israel, *Annual Report, 1961*, p. 157.
14. *Igerret Lahaverim*, January 5, 1961, p. 8.
15. *Al Hamishmar*, May 10, 1961, p. 1.
16. *Mibifnim*, November 1961, p. 25.
17. *Shituf*, March 1963, p. 25.
18. *Ibid.*, p. 27.
19. Zweig, *The Israeli Worker*, p. 226.
20. *Jerusalem Post*, March 29, 1963, p. 1.
21. *Bakibbutz*, May 8, 1963, p. 2.
22. *Hashavua Bakibbutz Ha'artzi*, March 22, 1963, p. 1.
23. Bank of Israel, *Annual Report, 1961*, pp. 157–158.
24. *Davar*, April 19, 1962, p. 2.
25. *Ha'aretz*, July 10, 1962, p. 18.
26. *Hashavua Bakibbutz Ha'artzi*, June 15, 1962, p. 8.
27. Shatil, *Economy*, pp. 202–203.
28. Audit Union, *Yediot*, September 1953, p. 3.
29. Shatil, *Economy*, p. 205.
30. *Ibid.*, p. 210.
31. S. Rosen, "The Kibbutz Movement," *Hedim*, July 1958, p. 40.
32. Darin-Drabkin, *The Other Society*, p. 362.

33. A. Rand, "Kibbutz Living Standards," *Hedim*, April 1959, pp. 49–51.

34. *The Economist* (London), May 16, 1959, p. 24.

35. *Business Diary*, July 26, 1962.

36. H. Darin-Drabkin, *Patterns of Cooperative Agriculture in Israel* (Jerusalem, 1962), p. 62.

37. *Al Hamishmar*, March 25, 1963, p. 4.

38. *Mibifnim*, June 1960, p. 346.

CHAPTER V: EFFICIENCY AND PRODUCTIVITY

1. Theodore W. Schultz, *Production and Welfare of Agriculture* (New York, 1949), p. 17.

2. *Jerusalem Post*, January 11, 1963, p. 3.

3. *Business Diary*, June 6, 1963, p. 125.

4. A. L. Gaathon, *Capital Stock: Employment and Output in Israel* (Jerusalem, 1961), p. 30.

5. Z. Abromowitz, "Advantages of Large Farms," *Lamerhav*, March 23, 1960, pp. 10, 11.

6. H. Nachshon, "The Cooperatives and Collectives in Israel," *Rivon Lekalkala*, March 1963, p. 102.

7. Audit Union, *Census of Production, 1964* and Government of Israel, *Statistical Abstract, 1964.*

8. Audit Union, *Yediot*, July 1962, pp. 9, 26.

9. Darin-Drabkin, *The Other Society*, p. 268.

10. The Falk Project for Economic Research in Israel, *Fifth Report 1959 and 1960*, p. 179.

11. *Horowitz Committee Report*, p. 52.

12. Audit Union, *Yediot*, July 1962, p. 16.

13. Raanan Weitz, *Agriculture and Rural Development in Israel: Projection and Planning*. The National and University Institute of Agriculture (February 1963), pp. 34, 35.

14. Audit Union, *Yediot*, July 1962, pp. 12, 13.

15. Bank of Israel, *Annual Report*, 1962, p. 150.

16. *Ibid.*, p. 126.

17. Hakibbutz Ha'artzi Federation, "Labor Force Summaries" (February 1965), p. 13.

18. Weitz, *Agriculture and Rural Development*, p. 41.

19. Darin-Drabkin, *The Other Society*, p. 269.

20. *Economic Report of the President* (Washington, January 1963), pp. 255, 259; Audit Union Reports on Agricultural Production; and Labor Force Surveys of the Central Bureau of Statistics.

21. Darin-Drabkin, *The Other Society*, pp. 280, 281.

CHAPTER VI: THE PROFITABILITY OF THE KIBBUTZ ECONOMY

1. Shatil, *Economy*, p. 378.

2. Audit Union, *Yalkut*, December 1957, p. 11; *Yediot*, June 1959, p. 33.

3. Gershon Kaddar, "The Profitability of Agriculture." Pamphlet issued by the Bank Leumi Le-Israel Ltd. (Tel Aviv), April 1958, p. 12.

4. *Hashavua Bakibbutz Ha'artzi*, July 28, 1961, p. 2.

5. Baruch Ber, "Kibbutz Losses," *Ha'aretz*, May 23, 1958, p. 2.

6. Falk Project, *Third Annual Report, 1957*, p. 35.

7. I. Shatil, "Economic Problems of the Kibbutz," *Hedim*, April 1960, pp. 57–58.

8. Audit Union, *Yalkut*, December 1957, p. 2.

9. Hakibbutz Ha'artzi Federation, "Labor Force Summaries" (March 1960), p. 34.

10. *Ibid.* (February 1965), p. 5.

11. Lowe, *Agricultural Economics*, pp. 279–281.

12. *Horowitz Committee Report*, p. 31.

13. *New York Herald Tribune*, June 14, 1960, p. 3.

14. Zev Zur, "Kibbutz Finances," *Mibifnim*, June 1960, p. 347.

15. Lowe, *Agricultural Economics*, p. 231; *Hedim*, April 1960, p. 58; *Mibifnim*, June 1960, p. 450.

16. Raanan Weitz, *Our Way in Agriculture and Settlement* (Tel Aviv, 1958), p. 254.

17. Kaddar, "Profitability of Agriculture," p. 24; *Horowitz Committee Report*, p. 33.

18. Raanan Weitz, "Problems of Profitability in Agriculture," *Davar*, June 18, 1958, p. 3.

19. *Horowitz Committee Report*, pp. 27–28.

20. E. Sadan, "Inputs and Outputs in the Kibbutzim," *Rivon Lekalkala*, November 1962, p. 402.

21. I. Shatil, "Mathematical Formulas and Reality," *Rivon Lekalkala*, March 1963, p. 172.

22. Yosef Fikman, "Strength of the Agricultural Economy," *Al Hamishmar*, June 15, 1960, p. 4.

23. *Horowitz Committee Report*, pp. 258–259.

24. *Ibid.*

25. *Ibid.*, pp. 146–147.

26. *Ibid.*, p. 131.

27. Yehuda Lowe, "Kibbutz and Moshav in Israel." An economic appraisal issued to the Ministry of Agriculture (Tel Aviv, August 1958), p. 6.

28. Rosen, "An Uncompleted Mission," p. 2.

29. Lowe, "Kibbutz and Moshav," p. 7.

30. A. Argov, "Greater Production and Productivity," *Bakibbutz*, February 25, 1959, pp. 1–3.

31. *Horowitz Committee Report*, p. 44.

32. Rosen, "An Uncompleted Mission," p. 2.

33. *Davar*, January 18, 1963, p. 9.

34. Weitz, *Our Way in Agriculture and Settlement*, pp. 142–143.

35. Bank of Israel, *Annual Report, 1961*, p. 181.

36. Kaddar, "Profitability of Agriculture," pp. 28, 35, 43.

37. *Mibifnim*, June 1960, p. 450.
38. Audit Union, *Yalkut*, December 1957, pp. 46–47.
39. Hakibbutz Ha'artzi Federation, "Labor Force Summaries" (March 1960), p. 34; (February 1965), p. 5.
40. *Bahistadrut*, May 1963, p. 59.
41. *Ha'aretz*, June 13, 1962, p. 6.
42. Yitzchak Oded, "Kibbutzim Need More Capital," *Business Diary*, January 20, 1960, p. 2.
43. Yair Kottler, "Kibbutz Members on Paper," *Ha'aretz*, September 7, 1962, p. 2.
44. Bank of Israel, *Annual Reports, 1959*, p. 44 and *1964*, p. 62.
45. *Israel Government Yearbook, 1962–1963* (Jerusalem, 1963), p. 344.
46. *Bahistadrut*, June 1963, p. 4.
47. Audit Union, *Population of Kibbutzim*, p. 19b.
48. *Ha'aretz*, July 11, 1963, p. 4.
49. Bank of Israel, *Annual Report, 1961*, pp. 151, 164, 165, 171, 172.
50. *Igerret Lahaverim*, August 15, 1963, p. 4.
51. Bank of Israel, *Annual Report, 1962*, pp. 157, 159, 161, 165, 167.
52. Moshe Zingerman, "The Kibbutz in all its Activities and all its Branches," *Bakibbutz*, March 5, 1965, pp. 5–6.
53. Bank of Israel, *Annual Report, 1964*, pp. 238–241.
54. Yosef Goell, "Kibbutz Industrial Output Equals Farm Production," *Jerusalem Post*, August 16, 1963, p. 3.
55. Shlomo Minsky, "With the Completion of the Second Million Jews in Israel," *Hedim*, April 1963, p. 72.
56. *Davar*, March 25, 1963, p. 8.
57. *Statistical Abstract, 1965*, p. 36.

CHAPTER VII: SUMMARY AND CONCLUSIONS

1. Minsky, "With the Completion," p. 72.
2. *Jerusalem Post*, July 26, 1963, p. 3.
3. *Ha'aretz*, July 31, 1963, p. 12.
4. Minsky, "With the Completion," p. 72.
5. *Hashavua Bakibbutz Ha'artzi*, January 18, 1963, p. 2.
6. *Ha'aretz*, July 13, 1965, p. 5.
7. *Ibid.*, August 16, 1965, p. 7.
8. Zvi Zinger, "The Crisis of Achievement," *The Jewish Horizon*, April 1963, p. 12.
9. Zalman Livneh, "Pioneers to the University," *Hashavua Bakibbutz Ha'artzi*, December 21, 1962, p. 1.
10. Emir Segev and Nachum Zvi Pesach, "Regional Cooperation: Shaar Hanegev"; *Hedim*, November 1964, p. 150.
11. Yosef Shatil, "Comments on the Economics of Collective Consumption," *Hedim*, April 1965, pp. 25–37.

GLOSSARY OF HEBREW AND TECHNICAL TERMS

Agricultural Year	The fiscal year used by most kibbutzim and other agricultural settlements, beginning with October 1 and ending September 30 of the following year.
Ahdut Ha'avodah	Israeli left-wing political party.
Branch	This term is used throughout the text to correspond with the Hebrew term "anaf," referring to a segment of the economy. In the kibbutzim, all economic activities, both of production and of consumption, are subdivided into branches.
Dunam	Land measurement = 0.247 acres.
Hahsharot	Training farms, outside of Israel, where prospective kibbutz members were prepared for their eventual participation in the kibbutz movement in Israel.
Haganah	The underground Jewish Armed Forces, during the period preceding the independence of Israel in 1948.
Hakibbutz Ha'artzi	A federation of kibbutzim, affiliated with the Marxist Mapam political party.
Hakibbutz Hadati	A federation of kibbutzim, affiliated with the Religious labor party, Hapoel Hamizrahi.
Hakibbutz Hameuhad	A federation of kibbutzim, affiliated with the Ahdut Ha'avodah party.
Hamashbir	Cooperative marketing organization, a subsidiary of the Histadrut, dealing with all products other than agricultural produce. The kibbutzim and most of the moshavim purchase the bulk of their supplies from this organization.
Ha'oved Hatzioni	A segment of the Progressive (moderate) political party (now known as "independent liberals").
Hapoel Hamizrahi	Religious labor party.
Histadrut	General Federation of Jewish Labor, to which the majority of the population in Israel belongs. In addition to trade union activities, it has established health, educational, manufacturing, and other institutions. Most of the kibbutzim and the moshavim are members of this federation.
Ihud Hakvutzot Vehakibbutzim	A federation of kibbutzim, affiliated with the socialist Mapai political party.

Israeli Pound (Lira) IL refers to the basic unit of Israeli currency. Until 1949 its official exchange rate was similar to that of the pound sterling, 0.248 to the American dollar. In 1949 it was devalued (along with the pound sterling) to 0.347 to the American dollar. In 1954 it was again devalued to 1.800 Israeli pounds to the American dollar. In fact, until 1962, the government had a system of multiple exchange rates. On the "Black Market" in Israel, or the "free market" abroad, the Israeli pound was sold at a very heavy discount. In 1950 the free market rate of exchange was about double the official rate. Prior to the official devaluation in 1954 the free market rate was almost seven times the official rate. During the period 1954 to 1962 when the official rate was 1.8 Israeli pounds to the American dollar, the free market exchange rate was between 28 per cent and 47 per cent higher. The average free market exchange rate in 1964 was IL 3,273 to the American dollar, i.e., 9 per cent higher than the official rate. Furthermore, the complex system of multiple exchange rate has been abolished since 1962 (though certain exported items are recipients of other forms of subsidization).

Jewish Agency The executive of the World Zionist Organization. Its members include representatives of some non-Zionist Jewish organizations. It concerns itself mainly with immigration and settlement in Israel.

Jewish National Fund A subsidiary of the World Zionist Organization, dealing with acquisition of land in Israel which it rents on the basis of long-term, low-rental renewable leases to kibbutzim, moshavim, and other Jewish groups in Israel.

Kibbutz Israeli collective or communal settlement.

Kibbutz Avodah Kibbutz preparatory groups, living near urban areas, awaiting settlement on the land. These groups were liquidated in the early 1950's, when the establishment of the State of Israel opened up many new areas for settlement.

Knesset Israel's parliament.

Kuppat Holim A subsidiary of the Histadrut, providing medical and hospital facilities for its members.

Mapai Socialist political party in Israel.

Mapam Marxist political party in Israel.

Mekorot	A company providing water for many settlements in Israel.
Metric Ton	1,000 kilograms or 2,204.6 pounds.
Moshav	An agricultural settlement based upon private family farms, with an agreement providing for many co-operative arrangements.
Moshav Shitufi	A settlement where all production is collective, similar to that in the kibbutz, but consumption — unlike the kibbutz — is on a family basis.
Nahal	Groups of soldiers who choose to spend most of their required National Service in a kibbutz. These groups are generally "graduates" of Israeli youth organizations affiliated with various kibbutz federations.
Palestinian Pound	It was the currency used in Palestine throughout most of the British Mandatory period. It was equivalent to the pound sterling.
Palmach	Special Units within the Haganah organization, consisting mostly of kibbutz members.
Po'alei Agudat Israel	A Religious (non-Zionist) labor party.
Tnuva	A subsidiary of the Histadrut engaged in marketing of agricultural produce. All kibbutzim and most of the moshavim are affiliated with Tnuva.
Yishuv	A term used when referring to the Jewish community in Palestine.
Yom Avodah	Literally, a work-day. Used in kibbutz accounting to designate the labor cost of the income-producing branches as defined by the ratio of the total number of work-days in kibbutz income-producing branches, divided by consumption expenditures in that kibbutz. It is also used to refer to the earnings per work-day in a particular income-producing branch as defined by the net income of that branch divided by the number of labor-days in that branch.
Youth Aliyah	A subsidiary of the World Zionist Organization, concerning itself with the immigration, education, and settlement of Jewish youth in Israel.